Tiny Homes
In a Big City

Reverend Faith Fowler

Cass Community Publishing House

For more information and further discussion, visit

CCPublishingHouse.org

Copyright © 2018 by Cass Community Publishing House

All Rights Reserved

ISBN: 978-1-942011-75-0

Version 2.0

Cover art and design by Richard DeRonne

For information about customized editions, bulk purchases or permissions, contact Cass Community Publishing House at 11745 Rosa Parks, Detroit, MI 48206 or ccumcac@aol.com.

In honor of Abbie Kay Reeves Malone McGowan,
who dedicated her life to social work,
and Eleanor Francis Fowler Hoag Frye,
who shared her life with the church.

Contents

Introduction

PEOPLE WHO WERE alive in 2001 know that Sept. 11 was a defining moment in time. Not since Pearl Harbor had the United States been attacked on its own soil by a foreign enemy. Not since the Revolutionary War had overseas adversaries killed almost 3,000 people on the mainland until terrorists crashed hijacked planes into the World Trade Center, a field in Stoney-creek Township, Pennsylvania and the Pentagon. On Sept. 12, the country had to adjust to a "new normal."

At Cass Community Social Services, our proverbial Sept. 11 occurred on Tuesday, Sept. 13. Innocent people didn't die and first responders didn't exhibit extraordinary heroism as they did on 9/11, but just as the country had had no forewarning about the shocking assault, the staff, board and residents at Cass were totally unaware of and unprepared for what was about to happen. A Californian named David Wolfe took and edited part of a video that one of our board members Karl Rausch produced about Cass' Tiny Homes. Our short film was created for an online fundraiser. Wolfe spliced out sections and added them to footage from a *Detroit News* video. Finally, he supplemented the two recordings with still shots and bolded block narrative. At

1:40 p.m., September 13, 2016, Wolfe uploaded "his" one minute, eight second video on Facebook.

We didn't know about the Wolfe video until it had over 2 million views. It went viral, skyrocketing to 6 million views within 10 days. (It continued to spread like wildfire so that by the new year, the number nearly doubled.) There were two problems with the post: first, Wolfe's text wasn't totally accurate. In fact, it was misleading. Therefore, feedback about our Tiny Homes project was skewed and much of it harshly criticized the program.

Second, an avalanche of people reached out to us with requests. Our website didn't crash, but it was impossible to keep up with the thousands of Facebook comments and messages, emails, voicemails, texts and letters. Nonprofits and government agencies sought to replicate the program in their cities. College and graduate students wanted to use the Tiny Homes community in their research projects. Hundreds of people contacted us to volunteer and hundreds more asked how to submit an application to live in one of the Tiny Homes.

The landslide of inquiries buried us. Our Tiny Homes weren't even finished (we had just completed one of the 25 houses in September). Our program was untested (we hadn't even selected tenants yet). There was serious fundraising and construction work still to be done and, so, time to respond was scarce.

We know that failing to reply to or acknowledge people who had taken the time to comment on David's Facebook post was rude. It was never our intention to ignore anyone. This book will answer many of the 6,000-some comments. It spells out our decision to build the Tiny Homes, provides a comparison with other organizations that have used tiny houses for people experiencing homelessness, explains the philosophy behind our plan and offers the logistics of building the homes—from the idea's infancy through occupation.

Each chapter will include some of the online feedback—positive, negative and questions. The posts are unaltered snapshots. The typos remain intact, as do the misspellings, bad grammar and run-on sentences.

Only the profile pictures were removed and we masked the last names as well as the offensive language. You will notice after a chapter or two that the themes repeat: homeless people are undeserving, drug addicted ... they should be required to help build the houses ... zoning makes Tiny Houses illegal ... Detroit is the worst place to attempt the program ... some argued the size of the Cass Tiny Homes was too small and others lamented that they are larger than their living areas in other countries ... countless other comments praised the idea. Here is a smorgasbord of the recurring themes:

Gayle ▓▓▓▓   Best idea I have seen in a long time
Like · Reply · September 14, 2016 at 12:01am

Lenora ▓▓▓▓   Great idea!!! But what help can people like me do to be able to afford to keep my house, we need a financial break as well.
Like · Reply · September 14, 2016 at 12:15am

Julie ▓▓▓▓   Having them help build these tiny house will also give them some labor and design skills ☺
Like · Reply · September 14, 2016 at 12:26am

Nathan ▓▓▓▓   Oh nice, another step towards communism. And anarchy soon enough.
Like · Reply · September 14, 2016 at 12:45am

Elias ▓▓▓▓   too bag the just banned tiny houses if u actually did ur research u would no that
Like · Reply · September 14, 2016 at 2:15am

Donald ▓▓▓▓   Go get a f██king job like me. I work my ass off just to pay rent.
Like · Reply · September 14, 2016 at 2:23am

Steve ▓▓▓▓   Future tiny crack houses.
Like · Reply · September 14, 2016 at 6:24am

Gillian ▓▓▓▓   Your small houses look big to most Brits!!!
Like · Reply · September 14, 2016 at 2:31am

Alex ▓▓▓▓   I'm from Spain and would love to take part on the project. How can I do so? Cheers!
Like · Reply · October 9, 2016 at 10:02am

Jacob ▓▓▓▓   What Detroit needs is a giant bomb! 💣💣💣 Boom!
Like · Reply · December 29, 2016 at 11:47pm

I didn't dignify the political tirades or the backlash against immigrants from the Facebook users by including them in the book.

In the end, it's hard to be mad at David Wolfe. Check him out on Wikipedia and you will discover that he cares about the environment, he advocates for a healthy diet that includes chocolate and he is the president of a nonprofit called the Fruit Tree Planting Foundation whose mission is to plant 18 billion fruit trees on the planet. And he, too, received negative comments:

Kyle ▓▓▓▓▓ You guys know just about everything posted by David Wolfe is bulls▓▓t, right?
Like · Reply · November 5, 2016 at 11:25am

In contrast to 9/11, Wolfe didn't attack us; he gave us exposure. His video catapulted our story across the United States and around the world. A London newspaper headline asserted that the Brits were "envious" of our Tiny Homes. A radio station in Malaysia invited us to appear on their show. People contacted us from Australia, Germany, Jamaica, Haiti, Canada, the U.K. and South Africa. Visitors came from across the continental U.S., too. We couldn't have paid for better advertising.

Moreover, Wolfe's post articulated the main idea: Tiny Homes in Detroit will allow formerly homeless people and other low-income individuals and couples to become homeowners. It is true that the compact homes are good for the environment. It is also accurate to see them as community revitalization. It is important that the project will put the properties back on the tax rolls, as well. They are good for Detroit as it rebounds from bankruptcy and tackles decades of population decline.

Still, for us, the most compelling reason to build Tiny Homes was to allow people trapped in poverty an opportunity to escape it by linking affordable housing to home ownership. For at least 25 formerly homeless adults, low-income senior citizens and college students, moving into one of the miniature houses was their defining day. A few arrived with just a plastic garbage bag stuffed with clothing and personal items. Keys to a home offered them instant privacy, security and dignity. For most, this was the first time in years that they were able to decide what to hang on the wall, what to store in the refrigerator, if and when company could visit, and whether they got to keep or own a pet. In seven years, if they work the program, the Tiny Homes will become theirs legally and indefinitely.

This book is meant to share the story with people, non-profits and government agencies that are considering a similar development. Hopefully, it will help them weigh the major considerations before putting a shovel in the ground: zoning, number of units, house size; type of housing, arrangement of the houses, foundations, infrastructure, governance, etc. The narrative talks about our rationale and the trade-offs for each decision. As for the Facebook users, we apologize that it has taken us so long to reciprocate. We believed that it was necessary for us to implement our ideas before sharing them.

Finally, the ultimate yardstick for the Cass Tiny Homes isn't how many people viewed or commented on David Wolfe's video. The real measurement of success will be determined by: how many people establish wealth by owning a (tiny) home, if an abandoned and blighted neighborhood starts to be repopulated and whether the program inspires others to build quality micro housing which will consume fewer resources, utilize less energy and emit substantially less CO_2.

—Rev. Faith Fowler

Cmarisol ▓▓▓▓ Great I'm happy but I been working 37 years and still don't own my home
Like · Reply · September 16, 2016 at 2:34pm

Elaine ▓▓▓▓ Seems like the american dream is just for some, and for others it's getting smaller
Like · Reply · September 14, 2016 at 7:20am

Sussan ▓▓▓▓ Love it ♥
Like · Reply · September 14, 2016 at 1:26pm

Jordan ▓▓▓▓ Sorry, but this is a fairytale
Like · Reply · September 16, 2016 at 10:31pm

1

The American Dream

"WHAT ARE HIS chances?" I heard my mother ask while holding the handset from the landline phone to her ear.

I understood from the expression etched on her face even if I couldn't hear the voice over the receiver that the prognosis wasn't good. I knew, too, not to ask about it once she replaced the device back into its tan cradle. She was sobbing and I was 6. Later I would learn that my maternal grandfather had been diagnosed with throat cancer. In those days, no one said the word cancer. They talked about the "c" disease because it was almost always fatal.

Fortunately, my grandfather was at Henry Ford Hospital on West Grand Boulevard in Detroit where oncology specialists were pioneering cutting-edge cancer surgeries. Doctors skillfully excised the malignant mass from his throat but also had to remove his vocal cords. I grew up knowing that my grandfather was a gifted orator but I never remember hearing his voice any louder than a whisper.

"What Are His Chances?" would have been an appropriate title for a book about his life. He was born in 1905 in East

Chicago, Indiana. He was the fourth of five children: Edward, Florence, Beatrice, my maternal grandfather, Charles, followed by Ralph, the baby of the family. His father was a railroad engineer and his mother was an osteopathic physician in Chicago, Illinois. Her medical skills couldn't save her son Ralph, who died as an infant, but when my grandfather contracted polio, she experimented with herbs and medicines until she helped him cheat death.

To be sure, the odds were stacked against him. Polio left him with limited use of one leg and a lifeless arm, which could be moved into place but otherwise dangled like a mannequin's limb. What's more, he had to drop out of school in eighth grade. Securing a job with physical handicaps and without a high school education made his future bleak.

Nonetheless, he was hired by a commercial cleaner. His job was to pick up and deliver laundry. One day, he got out of the Adelman Laundry truck in an alley and, while walking around the vehicle, he felt a pistol thrust into his rib cage. "Stick 'em up," demanded the less-than-original crook.

"I can't," he said.

The robber cocked his handgun. "**Do it now!**"

"I can't lift my left arm," he explained. Adrenaline was pumping through his bloodstream but he stood frozen in place. "I'm paralyzed."

What were the chances that the criminal would walk away? He did.

My grandfather met my grandmother, Abbie Mae Davis, at the cleaners. She was a laundry sorter. Originally from the very small town of Sorento, Illinois, she transplanted herself to Chicago for work at 18. Her apartment was down the street from Al Capone who, she said, always waved to her when he drove by. My grandparents were married in 1928. There was no honeymoon. They didn't have any money. The couple started their married life together in his parents' house.

During the Great Depression, my grandfather was out of work for six weeks until he landed a job in the food industry in Wisconsin. He told me once that it was a good move because no matter what happens with the economy, people still need to eat. He worked for a company called Zion Industries and later joined New England Products as a food broker. Eventually, my grandfather became the vice president of sales at Zion. At the New England Products building in Evanston, Illinois, he helped determine the ingredients for a new beverage named V8 vegetable juice.

His work caused him to move the Reeves family to Detroit. They rented a place on Lakewood. Unfortunately, in 1942, that house had a fire. It left their family, which by this time included three daughters—ages 13, 8 and 3—unhoused for five months while the repairs were done. They stayed with several relatives until they could move back into the house.

My grandfather's job required extensive traveling. One day in 1947 while on the road, a car plowed into his vehicle. A stranger held my grandfather's hemorrhaging head together while they waited for an ambulance. He spent eight weeks in the hospital and more than a year in rehabilitation. When he returned to work, the Detroit firm terminated his contract, his boss explained, because the scar on his forehead (caused by the collision) didn't fit their corporate image.

The settlement from the accident changed the trajectory of his career and the financial stability of his family. He opened his own business, the Charles Reeves Food Brokerage. He also became the president of the Detroit Association of Grocery Manufacturers Representatives (DAGMR). At 40, he purchased his family's first house. Two of his daughters went to college. Late in life, he and my grandmother invested in the stock market. Pepsi-Cola was their primary outlay (which dictated that my mother and I would have to hide our Coke and TaB cans in the bushes before entering their home).

He lived for 13 years after the cancerous tumor was removed from his throat. Together, my grandparents enjoyed traveling to Hawaii, China, Egypt, Europe and Russia. They took two ocean cruises around the world on the Queen Mary II. When he died in 1978, he left my grandmother financially secure and when she passed away nine years later, in 1987, their sizeable estate was divided between their three adult daughters.

I love his story. It reminds me that life was precarious two generations ago. Large numbers of women died in childbirth. Countless children contracted diseases that robbed them of a full life. The lucky ones who survived were often left challenged by the maladies and/or treatments. The story also speaks to my belief in tenacity and how with hard work one can overcome obstacles—polio, physical handicaps, a limited education, a criminal attack, unemployment, a house fire, a car crash and cancer. My grandfather's life story illustrates the power of the "pull yourself up by your bootstraps" American Dream. It "will preach" as they say. In this country, if you apply yourself you will be rewarded with a decent job, a good car, a nice house, retirement and travel. You will be able to share your gains with your children during your lifetime and you can pass on your wealth as an inheritance to them after your death.

The Cass Tiny Homes project is in large part a response to the fact that we live in a different time and that large numbers of people, despite amazing drive, resilience and hard work, do not experience comebacks or economic mobility. While polio no longer plagues the United States, poverty does. The combination of globalization and automation has radically changed and decreased the number of domestic jobs. Wages for those who have employment, when adjusted for inflation, have been stagnant for 40 years so that "working poor" is no longer an oxymoron. Incomes haven't kept pace with spiraling health care expenses or rising housing costs either. Student loans crush young graduates with debt. One in 5 children in the United States today lives below the poverty line. The majority will remain there.

The great "theologian" George Carlin joked, "It's called the American Dream because you have to be asleep to believe it."

During the 2016 Democratic primaries, Senator Bernie Sanders put a spotlight on income inequality. I would argue that asset disparity deserves an equal amount of scrutiny. Many people experiencing homelessness have traditional work and a large number of them do day labor or temporary jobs. Some of them have two jobs. What they don't have is a financial safety net. Thus, the problem for them and other low-income people occurs when they experience a crisis—someone becomes sick and is unable to work; someone's car breaks down and they are unable to get it repaired; someone's hours are reduced and they are no longer making enough to stay current with bills.

Without an asset, the poor can't borrow money unless they resort to businesses that practice predatory lending. Payday advances make loan sharks look like saints. They charge up to 400 percent interest and thus lock borrowers into a virtual debtor's prison. What's more, without an asset to serve as collateral, low-income individuals and families miss out on opportunities that present themselves such as enrolling in additional schooling or purchasing something that has been drastically discounted. Without wealth, debt is what poor people pass on to their families at the time of death.

Cass Community Tiny Homes are meant for low-income people—formerly homeless, senior citizens and college students who have aged out of foster care—who have established a regular source of income but lack a single asset. In particular, we wanted to provide a springboard for folks making as little as $9,000 a year for whom the American Dream was elusive at best. Our model was in sharp contrast to "Housing First" which provides people experiencing homelessness with housing before addressing their mental, physical, emotional and/or financial issues. The Cass program might be called "Home Ready," indicating that the program was designed for poor people who stand a high probability of succeeding as homeowners if they were given a chance.

Cass Community United Methodist Church and, later, Cass Community Social Services has worked with low- and no-income people for decades since the Great Depression. Both have provided meals, showers, shelter, laundry services, hygiene supplies, transitional and permanent supportive housing, as well as educational classes and employment to hundreds of thousands of people. We have celebrated over the years when individuals have beaten the odds but, more often than not, we have struggled with how to improve the chances for people mired in poverty.

The Cass Tiny Homes development is intended to help men and women who, like my grandfather, have so much to contribute but who, in stark contrast, have not been able to overcome multiple economic hurdles. We are convinced that facilitating their escape from poverty, the tar pits of our time, will have a positive impact on generations to come.

Above: Charles R. Reeves in a company truck.
Right: an early label from V8 vegetable juice—a product he helped develop and name.

Christina ▓▓▓▓ So many judgemental people. Nobody, as a child, decided they wanted to be homeless when they grow up. Something happened to them along the way. They travelled roads you know nothing about. Mental issues, histories of abuse, etc. Stop judging and start showing some empathy and compassion.
Like · Reply · September 14, 2016 at 6:55pm

Rose ▓▓▓▓ Sorry, But where do they PARK there Cars to Go to WORK??? Make a Big Shelter to Home Them, with Rooms! Not A house!! That is Not How they Make a living! That is How We As United States Support them!
Like · Reply · September 14, 2016 at 6:59pm

Marianne ▓▓▓▓ Let's see if they take care of them. If this turns out like the "projects' it will be good money thrown after bad. I believe everyone should have some 'skin in the game'.
Like · Reply · September 14, 2016 at 10:04pm

2

Nothing New Under the Sun

TINY HOUSES WEREN'T invented by Sarah Susanka (author of *The Not So Big House* in 1977) or Jay Shafer (founder of Tumbleweed Tiny House Company in 1979), although both thought leaders deserve gargantuan credit for popularizing the idea of living with less. HGTV programs and Pinterest have also raised awareness about the use of tiny houses. Nevertheless, small structures have been a part of the housing stock in the United States since the American Revolution. A review of the 1798 Federal Direct Tax returns for Massachusetts' Worcester County reveals that families lived in houses of only a couple of hundred square feet.[1]

Although few of the small houses have survived, the staff of Old Sturbridge Village in Massachusetts discovered the 1782-built, 420-square-foot house of blacksmith Jesse Rice buried under two additions in Brookfield, Massachusetts.[2] Jesse and his wife, Sarah Moore, had five children. In 1790, he added a 10-foot addition to the home. Unfortunately, his wife died in 1794 at the age of 35. Jesse married widow Mary Durham the next year. She had three children, so Jesse extended the house by

21 feet. Thus their family of 10 resided in a house measuring just 1,030 square feet.

Thoreau built his own "tiny" house by Walden Pond near Concord, Massachusetts.[3] The materials for the 10-by-15-foot cabin cost a mere $28.12 and he intentionally lived in the small, simple house from 1845 until 1847. The author wrote that he wanted to live "deliberately" in the one-room house. It was there that Thoreau penned works that inspired Mahatma Gandhi and Martin Luther King Jr. A replica stands in the original house's location in what is today a Massachusetts state park.

In addition to seeing the rocking chair in which President Lincoln was shot and the bus on which Rosa Parks refused to give up her seat, there is a replica of George Washington Carver's 12-by-12 cabin from Diamond Grove, Missouri in Greenfield Village at The Henry Ford in Dearborn, Michigan. Historians guess that Carver started living in the house in 1864. Since he was born into slavery, there is no record of his actual date of birth. The original home was destroyed by a tornado, but Henry Ford, using Dr. Carver's memories, recreated the structure to honor the famous botanist, chemist and inventor.

Ironically, as family sizes began to shrink over time, American houses were made larger with a few exceptions. First, tiny-sized houses were utilized in response to natural disasters such as the 1906 earthquake and fire in San Francisco. The quake and devastating fires destroyed 500 city blocks, leaving thousands of people unhoused. Initially, tents were pitched for the displaced population, but as the season changed union carpenters erected 5,610 shacks ranging from 140 square feet to 375 square feet.

The studio-style wooden shacks had unfinished interiors. They also lacked insulation and plumbing. There were wood and coal stoves for tenants who installed chimneys. Tenancy was reserved for people who had never owned a house before. At one time, 16,448 people resided in the buildings. The residents rented the shacks for $2 a month and their rent went toward the purchase price of $50 to $60. The only obligation was that people needed to live in the houses on the temporary site. Once they paid for the structures, they could be moved onto a lot somewhere else.

Democratic Architecture author, Donald MacDonald, noted that, "All but 267 of the shacks were sold and moved—sometimes piece by piece on their backs."[4]

Another example of tiny-sized houses used in response to a natural disaster occurred early in the 21st century. Following Hurricane Katrina and the floods that resulted from the breach of the levees, New Urbanist architects designed the 300-square-foot Katrina Cottage as an alternative to the FEMA trailers during a design charrette led by Andrés Duany. The attractive layout, small size and inexpensive price tag made the tiny houses a viable solution for the poor, displaced residents.

Moreover, tiny houses have been used by people experiencing economic emergencies throughout our national history. John Steinbeck wrote about them in his Pulitzer Prize-winning novel, *The Grapes of Wrath*.[5] Tom Joad, recently paroled from prison for homicide, hitchhiked home to discover that his family had vanished. He and his childhood pastor, Jim Casey, were alone in the house's dimly lit, dust-covered interior until an old neighbor Muley Graves entered and explained that the banks had evicted all of the area's sharecroppers. He told them, too, that Tom's family was temporarily staying nearby at his uncle John's farm.

The scenes from Uncle John's are jarring. A Caterpillar tractor bulldozed a house in a matter of seconds, rendering the building useless. The Joads decide to leave Oklahoma to go to California because they had seen handbills advertising good-paying jobs there. They sold their possessions for a pittance and used the money to buy a raggedy truck. What wasn't sold or burned was piled into the jalopy along with the former preacher and family members, including Rose of Sharon, a pregnant woman. Like many vehicles used by people experiencing homelessness today, the overloaded truck became their temporary home despite overheating, running out of gas, blowing a rod and a bald tire going flat…

As the fictional clan drove through the Southwest, Native Americans watched them along Route 66, reminding the readers that other people had been expelled from the land. Both the grandfather and grandmother died en route. As with legions of poor people, neither received a proper burial. Finally, the Joads crossed the border into California. Once they reached their destination, they quickly learned that too many dispossessed workers had responded to the handbills and thus wages were substantially lower than advertised. What's more, they were sent to a "transient camp" where the conditions were appalling. John Ford's movie based on the 1939 book shows a panoramic view of the squalor of the camp.

Reading *The Grapes of Wrath* was my first exposure to a tent city. I remember thinking even in high school that the conditions in the camp made the problems on the road seem miniscule. Hunger was pronounced. The camp children had to scrounge for food. They played on a garbage heap. There were no sanitary facilities. You could gag just thinking about the foul odors in the air. Steinbeck's classic book and Ford's controversial film won sympathy for people living in the tent encampments even though it concentrated on migrant workers.

Public approval for tent city inhabitants and their settlements has swung back and forth like a pendulum over time. "Squatter's camps" or "jungles," as they were called early on, trace all the way back to after the Civil War when men known as "hobos" and "tramps" rode the expanded railroad system.[6] The unhoused would retreat to the out-of-the-way areas where they could still be close to transportation, food, water and wood. The small colonies afforded them a place to wash up, eat and rest. They slept in tents or shacks they constructed themselves out of junkyard materials like tarps, cardboard and scraps of wood, cloth and tar paper. More than just refuge, the encampments provided a level of safety, privacy and community. Newcomers were welcomed and neighbors imparted survival techniques.

It is true that there were some lodging houses available for poor people but, as now, some folks were reluctant to use them. After 1929, however, "charities" were overwhelmed by the sheer volume of individuals and families who were newly destitute. Hence, more and larger jungles were pitched during the Great Depression. As Steinbeck mentions, in the 1930s the camps were called "Hoovervilles" because Herbert Hoover's name became synonymous with the country's financial disaster. Charles Michelson, the publicity chief of the Democratic National Committee, coined the derogatory term. People blamed the Republican president for letting the economy decline.[7]

Hoovervilles became common across the United States in the 1930s. Gwendolyn Mink and Alice O'Connor pointed out that several were well-documented and recognized. For instance, the one in New York's Central Park was originally called Hooverville Town.[8] When the stock market crashed in 1929, the reservoir north of Belvedere Castle was out of commission. A few homeless people took possession of the drained pool but the police quickly closed the camp. The homeless men returned and, because public sentiment had turned in their favor, they were allowed to remain there.

The buildings were exposed but tolerated by the general population—even those living in the luxury apartments surrounding Central Park. Photograph permission purchased from gettyimages. The picture is from from the New York Daily News Archive.

Soon the reservoir, renamed Hoover Valley, had a number of shacks. Some were unsophisticated and others were quite impressive. Unemployed brick builders constructed a shack with a roof that included inlaid tiles. A few utilized stone blocks from the reservoir itself. One of these shanties ended up being 20 feet tall. Twenty-nine men were living in 17 shacks in 1932, but the encampment disappeared in 1933 when work resumed on the reservoir.

Washington state had dozens of Hooverville shantytowns, including one of the largest and longest-lasting in the country.[9] There was a total of eight in Seattle, the biggest of which was located on vacant shipyard property of the Port of Seattle. It was started in 1931 by an unemployed lumberjack from Texas named Jesse Jackson. He and 20 other men began building shacks out of bits and pieces of wood and tin on top of the deserted concrete machinery pits. They erected 100 shacks in 30 days for homeless men. Then, the Department of Health and Sanitation raised hygienic concerns and posted seven-day eviction notices. At 5 a.m. on the seventh day, in torrential rain, law enforcement officers moved in and ignited the tent city after dosing it with kerosene. When the police left, the men returned and rebuilt the burnt-out shanties.

A month later, the police torched the primitive buildings a second time. Jackson and the other men decided to change their strategy. They designed a fireproof shack. The builders dug down into the cement pits, employing makeshift shovels. Then they covered the underground shanties with tin and steel roofs. Jackson served as a liaison between the city and the residents until finally, in 1932 under a new administration, the Health Department relented and allowed them to stay on the condition that they would comply with health and safety rules. One of the concessions was that the "gopher" structures needed to be replaced with above-ground shacks.

By 1934, nearly 500 small shelters were informally arranged at Seattle's main Hooverville. According to Donald Roy, a sociology graduate student at the time, there were 639 residents living there in March of that year and all but seven were men.[10]

Above: Tent city residents searching for food. Photograph is the property of the Museum of History & Industry. Used with permission. Below: The fires set by police caused the people to move underground. The photograph is from the Tacoma Public Library. Used with permission.

(One of the city's building and sanitation rules was that women and children weren't allowed to live in the Hooverville.) It was a diverse population according to Roy. Whites comprised 71 percent of the residents but people of color included Filipinos, African-Americans, Mexicans, Native Americans, South Americans and Japanese. Most were chronically unemployed laborers and timber workers

Jesse Jackson became the de facto mayor of the encampment. In 1938 he wrote a short description of life in the tent city.[11] It vividly recounted the initial hostility of local businesses, the development of an integrated Vigilance Committee (rule-making, enforcing body) and the simple nature of the shacks (no electricity, no heat, no running water, etc.). Jackson also described how the residents built pushcarts to collect waste materials from the city's alleys which were sorted, baled and sold.

As is true today, the census swelled during the winter months, reaching as high as 1,200 people according to Jackson. His Hooverville remained open from 1931 until 1941, when the land was reverted back to a shipping area prior to World War II.

There were other sizeable and significant camps in Los Angeles, Chicago, Portland and Washington, D.C. St. Louis, Missouri had a huge Hooverville along the banks of the Mississippi River just south of the St. Louis Municipal (later renamed MacArthur) Bridge in the 1930s.[12] Reports indicate that 5,000 people lived there. They were divided into four sections which were racially segregated. The community had an unofficial mayor, Gus Smith. Smith also served as the pastor. The location was viable until 1936 when the federal Works Progress Administration (WPA) "allocated slum clearance funds for the area."

The mood soured in the late 1930s. States began to increase residency requirements for poor people, making transients ineligible for assistance. As referenced in John Steinbeck's book, some states began using force to keep homeless people out. Then in 1941, a shack elimination program was introduced and numerous tent cities were demolished. As World War II approached, homeless men enlisted in the military and both genders secured employment in the assembly plants. Gradually, regular paychecks meant that they could secure apartments and—with the help of the GI bill—homes. Homelessness wouldn't steal the national spotlight again until the late 1970s and early 1980s when a sluggish economy, deregulation, deinstitutionalization and gentrification created an economic tsunami.

Beginning in the mid-1970s, the number of people experiencing homelessness started to climb rapidly once more and encampments returned to scores of urban areas. The tent cities tended to be small—a handful of people—and hidden, like Camp Take Notice in Ann Arbor, Michigan. Two of the larger settlements were the Justiceville camp on Skid Row in Los Angeles and Tompkins Square Park on the Lower East Side of Manhatten. Justiceville lasted a mere five months in 1985 but Tompkins Square Park operated for seven years. Both were forcibly dismantled by police.

Above: On December 14, 1989, police and park officials in riot helmets dismantled Tompkins Square Park in reaction to complaints from residents of the Lower East Side neighborhood. The photograph was taken by Robert Arihood. Permission to use the picture was granted by his brother, Leslie.

Aggressive removal tactics resulted in a general retreat from public spaces. Some people experiencing homelessness adopted a "mole" existence underground in the subway tunnels or in vacant structures along the rail lines. Others hid along the freeways and under bridges. The Oprah Winfrey Network aired *Tent City U.S.A.*, a documentary that depicted a homeless bridge community in Nashville, Tennessee.[13] The film crew shadowed several of the 80-plus residents for a few months.

One of the main "characters" in the film was Wendell, an unemployed carpenter who had built his own wooden 8-by-12-foot house which was filled with amenities—a television, a refrigerator, a toaster oven and a laptop hooked up to the Internet. Wendell also erected a community shower complete with on-demand hot water.

Another Nashville tent city resident is shown helping a new arrival assimilate. He taught the woman how to make a "no-installation-charges, no-monthly monitoring-fees alarm system" by piling twigs in a circle around her tent. The video also introduces a couple from Kentucky who, among other things, persuaded a salesman at a resale shop to drop the price of a wedding dress to $7 so they could purchase it with their savings.

The documentary singles out two pastors from the Otter Creek Church of Christ. Their congregation played a key role in cleaning up the encampment. Moreover, Rev. Doug Sanders and Rev. Jeannie Alexander, formerly a corporate attorney, worked as advocates with the men and women of the camp. When the landowner (the Tennessee Department of Transportation) shared its plans to rehab the bridge above the camp, the clergy assisted with a search for new property. Unfortunately, the life-threatening floods of 2010 submerged the area in 10 feet of water before a new home could be identified. The pastors were instrumental in helping to relocate the uprooted people to private land, respond to the neighborhood's NIMBY (Not In My Back Yard) reaction, connect with the Homelessness Commission and campaign for political inclusion.

The documentary challenges many of the stereotypes people have about mental illness, drug and alcohol abuse, and laziness as the cause(s) of homelessness. It likewise raises important questions about the use of government vouchers and the role of case management. The video captures the success of several residents but the documentary ends abruptly, unfinished. No replacement tent city had been identified or sanctioned and the private land they occupied after the flood was limited to six months. The film concludes that unsanctioned encampments were sprouting up across Nashville.

Other cities from Camden, New Jersey to Seattle, Washington, from Reading, Pennsylvania to Los Angeles, California, from Las Cruces, Minnesota to Austin, Texas have had tent cities during the last couple of decades. Some have been bulldozed or otherwise evicted such as Camp Take Notice in Ann Arbor. Some have been itinerant like SHARE/WHEEL'S sanctioned camps Nos. 3 and 4 in Seattle, which move every three months. Others have evolved into tiny house villages.

Katherine ████ They need to do that in L.A the homeless problem there is terrible.
Like · Reply · September 14, 2016 at 12:52am
Kristin ████ Salt Lake City did this first and rocked it!!!!They're pretty forward-thinking and all about community there; hope that spirit spreads to Detroit!!!!
Like · Reply · September 14, 2016 at 11:57pm
Tina ████ It is very interesting how they comment that Portland is solving homeless with tiny homes??? Am I missing something?
Like · Reply · September 16, 2016 at 11:47am

3

Tiny House Villages

IT WASN'T UNTIL the turn of the century that groups in the United States began using more permanent structures as a resource for people experiencing homelessness. The majority of the groups were protesting municipal ordinances (which increasingly outlawed individuals sleeping, smoking, loitering or food-sharing on public property). A handful of cities went so far as to prohibit sitting or lying down in public. In fact, some municipalities installed spikes on their public benches and tables to discourage loitering.

The National Law Center on Homelessness & Poverty released its 11th report on the criminalization of homelessness in 2014. "No Safe Place: The Criminalization of Homelessness in U.S. Cities" describes the alarming trend of new statutes that punished people living in public. Analyzing laws from 187 U.S. cities, the report is packed with statistics that illustrate the escalation of criminalization across the country. For example:

> In 2011, 70 cities banned sitting or lying down in public places. In 2014, the number jumped to 100 cities banning sitting or lying down in public places, a 43 percent increase in three years.
>
> In 2011, 37 cities banned sleeping in cars. In 2014, 81 cities banned sleeping in cars, a 119 percent increase.[14]

In *Tent City Urbanism*, author and urban planner Andrew Heben writes that tiny house villages often converted "places of protest into places of refuge."[15] He also observed that the design of the semi-permanent structures mirrored the pattern of tent cities with smaller sleeping spaces and larger common areas for gathering and cooking/eating. The tiny house villages copied the centralized toilets/bathing, as well. Heben contends that this physical layout allowed for community experiences that were missing from the grid street pattern most cities had adopted. Many of the 21st century villages would ultimately be sanctioned (allowed to exist on public or private property) versus the tent cities, which remained mainly unsanctioned (illegal). Following the tent cities pattern, the villages generally ended up in the outskirts of the city.

Dignity Village in Portland, Oregon (2004-present)

Dignity Village has the distinction of being the very first program in the country to use tiny houses for people experiencing homelessness. Like other urban areas, Portland created and implemented more than one 10-year plan to end homelessness. In fact, they were making significant progress on their third 10-year plan using a "housing-first" strategy when a recession stymied the local economy and city officials shifted funding that had been allocated for addressing homelessness to programs that focused on foreclosures.

Dignity Village was first established as a tent city in downtown Portland in December 2000. It was closed by city officials repeatedly and then the group, known as Camp Dignity, relocated to a parcel of land underneath a bridge. It was highly controversial at the time and, only after establishing a 501(c)(3) in 2004 and intense negotiations with the city, was it moved to city property in northeast Portland, where Dignity Village remains today. There are some concerns related to the parcel. Dignity Village is sandwiched between a leaf-composting plant and the Columbia River Correctional Institution. The first frequently produces a horrible stench and the state prison raises security issues. The village is also about a mile from the Portland International Airport so that jets fly overhead with some frequency. Therefore, the residents are exposed to fumes and noise pollution, as well.

Perhaps even more troublesome is that Dignity Village is located some 9 miles from downtown Portland. The distance caused some of the people living in the tent city to relocate elsewhere. Moreover, graduate student Catherine Mingoya observed that residents require two bus transfers and almost an hour to get to where most of the jobs and social service agencies are situated downtown.[16] There are no sidewalks or bike lanes.

Mingoya likewise noted in her graduate paper that the village is paved with impermeable blacktop which constantly floods because Portland has an inordinate amount of rain annually and the drainage system doesn't function properly. Add that to the reality that the village has only four porta-potties and a single propane-heated, outside shower to accommodate between 40 and 60 residents.

Nonetheless, adults experiencing homelessness apply to be admitted and there is a standing waiting list. They are drawn to the village because it provides independence and privacy. A few residents told me that they preferred the location because it was quiet. One rule that distinguishes Dignity Village from many other encampments that would follow is that children are not allowed since no criminal background screening is conducted. Residents/members pay the village $35 in monthly rent and they are required to volunteer 10 hours a week in one of the micro-enterprises (such as firewood collection or food carts) to pay for common utilities.

Tents were used first in the new Dignity location, but moveable, raised tiny house structures replaced them in time. There are 43 units (the maximum allowed by the city) constructed by both the residents and volunteers using donated materials. Given the age of the structures, some are showing signs of wear and tear. Deconstruction and renovation is an ongoing project. The day I visited, two volunteer crews were at work painting and doing carpentry on a couple of houses. A student group was also touring the village before they started to build a facility that would be used as a new computer lab. Building, maintenance and renovation costs are only a fraction of what would be required to construct a studio or one-bedroom apartment in the area. The Dignity Village houses cost a mere $3,000 while a small local apartment of approximately the same size has a price tag of more than $200,000.

The camp is self-managed and self-governed so that all of the rules and decisions are made by the members. They meet every other Tuesday night and they vote on policies like whether guests need to be escorted to the porta-potties in the middle of the night. One month they may restrict guest movement by a majority vote and the next they might reverse it by the same. They also resolve any conflicts between people and enforce consequences when rules have been broken.

All financial decisions are made by the village residents. For example, a high school service group sponsored a fundraiser and decided to donate a $500 Home Depot gift card to the village. There was an extensive discussion at a membership meeting about what the money should fund. Residents debated the merits of buying a chop saw for village use. In fact, they handle all things financial, insuring that the organization pays its bills: utilities, insurance, Internet, porta-potty service and storm water drainage fees.

Although the costs are roughly one-third of operating a traditional shelter in the Portland area, the village would benefit from additional income. For instance, if more money was available, Dignity could hook up with the municipal sanitation system and eliminate numerous health/hygiene concerns. They could install

DIGNITY VILLAGE *Above: As the oldest village, Dignity continually deconstructs and rebuilds its tiny houses. Notice the single solar panel, the tarps that protect outside belongings from the rain and the assortment of house sizes and colors. There is a grassroots and friendly feel to the community. It's a little cluttered with wood, recycling and gardening beds/tools not seen in the photo. The cats, not seen either, love it. Below: Just beyond a recycling section of the camp and Dignity's back fence, you can observe the piles of composting leaves.*

a water catchment system, too, with sufficient funding. One of the tradeoffs of DIY governance has been that the settlement doesn't fundraise in the traditional way. Most nonprofits with "outside" board members are better positioned to solicit money to help accomplish the mission.

Clearly the tiny houses were and are a vast improvement from living in tent cities, especially unsanctioned ones. People aren't forced to move abruptly. They don't lose their belongings as a result of police sweeps or leaky tents. The community is less fluid. The sanitation is improved. Volunteers play a beneficial role in the village without taking control. An on-site program specialist is available and engagement is voluntary.

There is still some fear that Dignity Village itself will be forced to move once more. Rumor has it that Sunderland Yard, managed by the Portland Bureau of Transportation (PBOT), would like more space to make fertilizer. According to the city of Portland website, they recycle 5,000 tons annually at present. Katie Mays, the program support specialist at Dignity Village, thinks that the village is relatively safe where it is because the current location costs the city little money. City officials now tout the program as an "innovative" success to visitors and the village has solid support from the Portland Housing Bureau and the Joint Office of Homeless Services. Identifying another site would almost certainly be a formidable challenge.

There is no consensus about what type of housing Dignity Village offers. Originally, the founders wanted to establish a community without time limits—real or perceived. Many people today classify the tiny homes as transitional, meaning that residents can stay for up to two years. Several of the people have been there much longer. Many of them would like to move on but they are stuck because there are long waiting lists for affordable housing. Also, the village initially didn't include staff to help residents navigate social services systems or complete complicated applications such as the one for Supplemental Security Income (SSI).

Opportunity Village in Eugene, Oregon (2013-present)

Opportunity Village began as a pilot project in 2013, but it grew out of an Occupy encampment that was organized in August 2011. With time, the housed activists were joined by up to 100 unhoused adults in the camp which provided food and shelter. The city relocated the Occupy camp several times until December 2011 when the encampment was closed due to a violent fight. Nevertheless, the proximity that protestors had to people experiencing homelessness in the camp raised their awareness of and their empathy for unhoused people.

Eugene's mayor, Kitty Piercy, appointed a task force to look for innovative ideas to address homelessness called Opportunity Eugene-A Task Force on Homelessness.[17] This task force included a wide array of representatives comprised of business owners, police officers, school administrators, nonprofit agencies and neighborhood organizations, as well as representatives from the camp. Committee meetings generated a number of recommendations. The most significant suggestion was that the city staff members should work with community members to identify potential sites for "a safe and secure place to be, open by October 1, 2012, independently financed with oversight by a not-for-profit organization or agency."

Advocates, many of whom had been involved in the Occupy camp, continued to meet informally. They became known as the Homeless Solutions Committee and they focused on the framework of establishing a self-governed, residential village for homeless people. Their initial proposal called for four small villages (each with approximately 30 tiny houses), but after listening to public feedback, the group limited their proposal to a single 30-unit pilot project. In January 2013, the city council passed a motion directing the city manager to locate a parcel of city owned property to be used for the micro-housing for homeless people.

The manager selected property in the Trainsong neighborhood. It was formerly a trailer park and the city had planned to utilize it for a storage facility. Since they didn't have the funds to proceed, they approved a temporary lease for the tiny house community, good for about a year if a conditional use permit could be obtained. Although the location is in a light industrial area, it is much closer to downtown than other villages. It is within walking distance to some services and just one block away from a bus stop. In fact, the board has arranged with the local Department of Transportation to purchase monthly bus passes at discounted rates. Thus, every resident is issued a free monthly bus card.

The village was given the green light to proceed on the property in August 2013. Residents, volunteers and skilled tradespeople built Opportunity Village over the course of the next nine months. The building costs were significantly less due to donated labor. They spent roughly $2,000 per house and $100,000 for the entire village using another $100,000 worth of donated materials and labor. The organization sponsored a "big build" during which volunteers and residents erected five houses, built 10 raised garden beds, and dug a 200-foot-long, 2-foot-deep trench to run the water lines for the proposed kitchen. Dan Bryant, the executive director of Opportunity Village and senior minister at the First Christian Church in Eugene, explained that if they had to do it over, he would recommend installing plumbing for the bathrooms right away. He said that at first they rented four porta-potties and the fees cost them a small fortune. The local Rotary Club contributed $4,000 to hook up a permanent bathhouse to the city water and sewer.

By May 2014, the village was built—a combination of 29 brightly colored tiny, 60- to 80-square-foot houses and Conestoga huts (built on pier blocks with wood platforms, hog wire, bubble wrap and foam insulation). The larger 8-by-10-foot houses are reserved for couples and single adults use the 8-by-8 models. Some of the houses have lofts for storage. The houses don't have electricity (with the exception of a few which rely on extension cords to power medical equipment) and they aren't heated. On cold nights many of the residents choose to sleep in the 30-foot communal yurt (a portable, round tent with a dome-style roof). It contains a pellet stove. During the daytime hours, residents take advantage of the yurt space for using the Internet-linked computers, watching a large-screen television or reading a book from the library.

The kitchen is outside next to the heated bathhouse which contains two toilets, one shower and laundry appliances in the back. Residents sign up for showers in half-hour shifts. The 50-gallon hot water heater has proved sufficient for this incremental schedule. It was thought at first that the residents would want congregate meals but they insisted that they wanted to cook for themselves. Therefore, each tenant has a plastic container in the shared refrigerator for storage. Opportunity Village is also a food distribution site. Thus, residents can receive donated food items every Tuesday and vegetables grown in a village garden. The closest grocery store is roughly half a mile away and a convenience store is available at the end of the street.

Occupy Eugene changed its name to Opportunity Village when the nonprofit SquareOne Villages was formed. The transitional housing program adopted just five rules:

1. No violence.
2. No theft.
3. No alcohol or illegal drugs on-site.
4. No persistent, disruptive behavior.
5. Everyone must contribute to the operation and maintenance of the village.

Residents are expected to volunteer 10 hours a week in addition to paying $30 monthly rent. They staff the single entrance 24/7. Although the program doesn't require sobriety, anyone entering the village high or under the influence of alcohol is told to go to his/her house. Disruptive incidents have been minimal. The camp had a loud episode with an intoxicated resident on the very first night, but it was handled quickly and appropriately and served as an example.

When someone seeking housing comes to the security gate, that person is asked to complete an application. Then, a vetting committee, composed of three residents and one board member,

OPPORTUNITY VILLAGE Above: There are two sizes of tiny houses and some smaller Conestoga huts. Everything is brightly colored and residents personalize the interiors and exteriors of the houses. All of the houses use pier blocks to lift them off the ground. Below: Beyond the outside dining area, a large yurt serves as a community gathering space and, in extreme weather, as a heated sleeping area for those who want to escape their unheated houses.

interviews the person to decide whether Opportunity Village would be a good fit. Accepted candidates go onto a short waiting list. Inclusion on the list allows them privileges even before moving into the village. They can come in and take showers. They are allowed to sleep in the yurt. This helps with the assimilation process and it facilitates keeping track of people until they can become residents.

Opportunity Village hasn't had a paid staff. The original philosophy was to connect residents with resources in the larger community. Recently, they decided to bring on a college intern who will have the responsibility of creating a transition plan with each resident. In terms of governance, Opportunity Village is self-managed and self-governed but it works hand-in-glove with the nonprofit, SquareOne Villages, which includes a couple of residents and members of the surrounding community. SquareOne has the responsibility of insuring that the program remains compliant with the city contract.

At some time in the future, the city expects to expand the public works plant, which would impact the 1 acre that the village is occupying. It is doubtful, however, that this will happen soon. The leases have been renewed with little to no opposition. An October 2015 community planning report associated with the University of Oregon evaluated the effectiveness of Opportunity Village.[18] Among other things, the 93-page document spelled out that the residents were substantially satisfied with their lives in the village and the community viewed the residential program favorably, as well. Ninety percent of the neighboring residents and businesses indicated that they were supportive of the village. (The most frequent suggestion from the residents was to enlarge the kitchen.)

Quixote Village in Olympia, Washington (2013-present)

Quixote Village evolved from a tent encampment known as the Poor People's Union that was organized in Olympia in early 2007.[19] When the city threatened to expel the camp, a local Unitarian Universalist parish offered to host the homeless group in its parking lot. The camp was protected there due to the provisions in both the federal and state constitutions, which provide for the freedom of religion. Next, Olympia passed the "Temporary Homeless Encampments" ordinance which mandated that someone from the church must be onsite 24/7 and that the camp must be removed every 90 days. Over time, seven religious communities volunteered to "host" the rotating group named Camp Quixote.

The camp was composed of roughly 30 adults. All of the members belonged to the resident council, which had the responsibility of determining the rules and deciding who to admit and when to evict a resident. Furthermore, the council elected officers, who had the authority to conduct business between meetings. The self-governance model was so successful that the city of Olympia extended the time the camp could remain at a site to 180 days. Even with the extended time frame, Camp Quixote relocated more than 20 times in seven years.

Panza, a nonprofit named after Sancho Panza, Don Quixote's faithful servant, was formed by some of the volunteers from the host churches. It adopted the mission of locating land and building a permanent place for the camp. A 2.17-acre county-owned parcel was identified in an industrial park at the edge of Olympia, bordering the neighboring city of Turnwater. Panza negotiated a 41-year lease for $1 a year from Thurston County for the property. The move made Panza the landlord and turned Camp Quixote into Quixote Village. The new relationship also diminished some of the involvement of the resident council in decision-making.

Garner Miller, an architect by trade and an active volunteer at Camp Quixote, consulted with the camp residents in order

QUIXOTE VILLAGE Above: In an assortment of earth-toned colors, 30 identical cabins encircle the water retention ponds. In the background is the trucking company building. Below right: Each house has a charming porch. Below left: This is the front page news article about Camp Quixote's eviction. Community Frameworks served as the project manager and the fiscal agent for the new village development.

to establish a design scheme. They decided to use tiny houses (144 square feet) and a shared building for bathing and cooking. Originally, the plan didn't include plumbing in the houses but, responding to feedback, they soon added a half bath in each unit so that people wouldn't have to dress to go outside to use the restroom. Consultation with the residents also resulted in front porches and the arrangement of Camp Quixote's 30 identical tiny houses clustered around water retention ponds, facing the attractive 4,000-square-foot community building at the village's entrance.

Unlike nearly all of the other villages, funding for the construction and operations of Quixote came primarily from government sources: The Washington State Housing Trust Fund, the Department of Housing and Urban Development (HUD), the City of Olympia and Thurston County. A white paper (an authoritative informational report on proposals or issues) about Quixote Village by Ginger Segel indicates that the capital funding required exceeded 3 million dollars and that a fraction of the total cost (just over $300,000) came from private contributions.[20] Roughly two-thirds of the budget paid for site work and construction. Due to funding source requirements, only professionals were used to construct the buildings and the labor costs were exorbitantly high because they had to pay the prevailing commercial wage rates. The land and title cost another $337,000 and architectural and engineering costs came in at $208,397.

The operating budget is also generated almost exclusively from government grants. The annual income is roughly $250,000 according to the white paper. In addition to covering insurance, repairs and maintenance, and the audit, the income pays for two full-time staff, a program manager for operations and a case manager who helps residents obtain social services. Since Quixote Village is a HUD-funded program, residents pay one-third of their monthly income as rent. Tenant rents for non-Section 8 units generate about $6,000 annually.

Residents of the permanent supportive housing village moved in before the end of 2013. One of the residents recalled nostalgically that he had gone outside to go to the restroom on

Christmas Eve and a staff person needed to remind him that there was a toilet and sink inside his house. People used to living in tents learned to enjoy the heat and electricity in their houses. There were other adjustments, as well. One is the mandatory drug testing. (Quixote banned illegal drugs from its opening day and added a ban on alcohol later. Marijuana is allowed since it is legal in Washington.) Finally, residents had to deal with the 4-mile distance to Olympia, Washington's state capital.

Occupy Madison in Madison, Wisconsin (2014-present)

The entire country was captivated by the 2011 Occupy Wall Street movement in Manhattan. On October 7, 2011, Occupy Madison was born in Reynolds Park as activists gathered to show solidarity with demonstrators across the country. They willingly moved their encampment to Veterans Plaza when neighbors complained later that same month. In November, they were displaced once more to accommodate Freakfest, Madison's Halloween music festival, and the protestors landed in Monona Terrace. Next, also in November, the camp relocated to 800 East Washington at the suggestion of the city. The protestors applied for and received a permit from the city of Madison, a progressive college town, which allowed them to form a temporary tent encampment.

Soon, the Occupy Madison parking lot encampment started attracting more and more homeless individuals in addition to the activists. Both groups utilized the tents, shared the food and participated in meetings. According to co-founder Allen Barkoff, this was the organizers' first real encounter with people experiencing homelessness.[21] During the following months of brutal winter weather, the Occupy leadership worked with the fire department, the health department, the police department and the mayor's office to address an endless list of costly corrections. They also responded to recommendations from multiple municipal inspections.

Dispersal orders began routinely arriving after the first of the year because the city's permit was set to expire. The protestors, in utter frustration and wanting to garner media attention, decided to relocate the camp to the lawn of the city's Health and Human Services office. After 10 days, the sheriff's department physically dismantled the encampment using dump trucks. They moved the people and their belongings to Token Creek County Park, some 2 miles outside of town and 7 miles from the nearest bus stop. Allen Barkoff said the encounter felt "like a narcotics raid and was very militaristic."[22]

Some supporters stepped in, bringing the people food and heaters, but the park flooded and froze more than once and the campers were miserable. Like Quixote, they would be forced to shuffle repeatedly. The campground kept adding new rules so that at one point, residents had to relocate every 14 days for at least two days at a time. Each move was difficult physically, financially and emotionally. In 558 days, the settlement changed locations 30 times. A citizen, Koua Vang, allowed them to live on his private property during the spring months when the campgrounds were closed, but he was threatened with excessive fines ($300 a day) for breaking zoning laws so the people left his land, too.

Finally, in May 2012, the group gave up on their attempts to comply with the city's restrictions and ordinances. They decided, although no one can remember who presented the idea, to create a tiny house village. The thought was that the small mobile shelters could be moved around Madison without breaking any parking laws—the tiny houses could fit into a regular parking space—and, at the same time, they would publicize their issues. Bruce Wellbaum, Occupy Madison treasurer, found out, too, that if they didn't weigh more than 3,000 pounds, the houses weren't required to be registered.[23]

It took months to identify a property that Occupy Madison could buy. They ultimately purchased an old gas station turned auto repair shop that was on the market. Then, they started a campaign to gain approval from the city aldermen (council members), to use the lot for the village. Public approval was neither automatic nor quick. Fortunately, Brenda Konkle, a former alderman, lawyer, planning commissioner and executive director of the city's tenant resource center was also a co-founder of Occupy Madison Village. She strategically ushered the project through the process, which included crowded neighborhood meetings. Some of the neighbors objected to the negative impact they believed the village would bring (recurring NIMBY concerns such as plummeting housing values and an increase in crime). Konkle answered their questions, interacted with city representatives including the police chief and ensured that Occupy Madison communicated information and updates on the web. Future residents also paved the way by speaking at a number of "meet and greet" events. Neighbors were much more empathic once they heard some of the personal stories and put names and faces with people.

A number of other stakeholders played significant roles with the development. Several founding members pooled their resources to loan the project $75,000 as a down payment and helped secure a mortgage from a local credit union in order to purchase the lot for $110,000. Occupy Madison closed on the property in May of 2014. An area architect played a key part, as well. He reviewed the original Google sketch design that crammed as many houses as possible into the available space and, after conferring with concerned local residents, he modified the layout so that only nine homes would curve around the former auto repair shop/community building. The smaller number proved to be less threatening to the surrounding community.

Volunteers installed a richly colored brick walkway connecting the houses and the main building. Only the tops of the houses are visible from the street because the perimeter of the property is defined by a decorated wooden stockade-style fence which provides privacy and security. Each 98-square-foot building (five of the nine houses were up and occupied in March 2017) is brightly painted, resembling some of the houses in the community with their pitched roofs and shuttered windows. All of the houses are on trailers to avoid the city's minimum-size standards. Each house has electricity and heat. The neat and tidy courtyard has raised flowerbeds and an assortment of parked

OCCUPY MADISON *Above: The houses at Occupy Madison angle inward so that residents enjoy more sunlight and the colorful exteriors of the collection of tiny houses. After the third house, new shells were built by a construction class at La Follette High School. Below: Some of the products made by residents in the woodshop are displayed in the sales space. Income from OM Goods supports the operating budget of the village.*

bicycles even though the residents have immediate access to the bus lines directly across the street.

Village applicants must complete 32 hours of work in order to move in. Residents continue to contribute 10 hours of volunteer time per week until they reach 500 hours. Once they have accumulated 500, the village considers their houses "paid-off" but they must still give 10 hours per week to help maintain the village and/or to assist with the nonprofit's micro-enterprise. Residents working in OM Goods recycle materials to produce furniture, planters, birdhouses, candle holders, signs, etc. in the woodshop that is located in the former auto station. This retro-fitted building also houses the sales room for their goods and Occupy Madison T-shirts, hats and postcards; three bathrooms; a staff office and a modest, makeshift kitchen.

Income from sales is essential to the operations of Occupy. The $77,000 mortgage and $160,000 for the installations and renovations of the common building plus approximately $200 a month for utilities demands a regular infusion of cash. The non-profit hasn't been successful in attracting grants to date but they have leveraged media coverage to solicit donations. Thousands of readers shared a story from Al Jazeera America about the grand opening and a post on US Uncut's Facebook page was shared more than 170,000 times. One of the first residents was proud of the fact that his name appeared in the *Moscow Times* even if he grew weary of interviews and tours. When *Star Trek* actor George Takei posted a photo of the village's ribbon-cutting ceremony on his Facebook page, the picture received 36,678 likes and was shared more than 6,000 times.[24] Eight million people were exposed to the image and Occupy Madison received $16,000 in one week.

The board of directors is composed of 13 volunteers, a mixture of outside supporters and village residents, with diverse backgrounds and professional experience. They handle financial management, fundraising, volunteering and municipal compliance using a consensus model. Even though the organization doesn't receive government grants (wanting to remain independent), they have been responsive to regulations. For instance, they conformed to ADA standards by constructing an accessible bathroom.

Second Wind Cottages in Ithaca, New York (2014-present)

The tiny houses in Newfield, New York were not created in reaction to shelter accommodations, the criminalization of homelessness or the Occupy movement. They went up because a man named Carmen Guidi read a book. After finishing *Radical* by David Platt in 2010, the auto mechanic signed up with a team for a short-term mission which took him to Haiti.[25] The trip changed his life. It was the first time he saw a dead body. It was an 8-year-old girl. When he returned home, Carmen got involved with the Red Cross Friendship Center in Ithaca. One day when he was volunteering at their soup kitchen, a homeless man told him that he slept under a bridge in "The Jungle."

Although Carmen was raised in Newfield, 5 miles south of Ithaca, like many other local people he was unaware of the oldest documented encampments in the United States. That's probably because you have to know where to look for the 100-year-old, unsanctioned camp. The settlement is tucked off of Ithaca's main commercial boulevard and behind a Walmart store. People enter the camp using a footpath that snakes through overgrown grass beside a wide creek. The homeless loom behind the thickets of trees. Most are men, clustered in tents and shacks made out of cardboard and trash. There is no electricity, no toilets or showers. The only heat is generated by propane stoves or campfires. In a video tour of The Jungle, Carmen mentioned the memorial decorations (wooden crosses, plastic flowers, posted pictures) that underscore that the natural setting can be a dangerous place.

Carmen brought his friends Don Reed and Jeff Teeter with him the first time he visited. They took food (pizza) and blankets. He returned again and again, sometimes alone and other times with his family. Eventually Carmen developed trusting relationships with the camp residents. When he came back home from a mission trip to Honduras in 2011, his wife told him that one of the men living in The Jungle had hung himself that morning. It was crushing news. That winter Carmen purchased eight campers. He started inviting people to stay on his property behind the auto shop. His efforts emptied The Jungle for Christmas in 2012. (It hadn't been vacated since World War II.) Although the campers were equipped with heat and water, they weren't ideal for upstate New York's brutal winters.

So, in 2013, Carmen persuaded his two companions to help him start building 16-by-20-foot winterized houses. The stand-alone "cottages" were like studio apartments with plumbing, electricity and a small kitchen. Twelve identical tiny houses have been built to date and 19 are anticipated at a cost of $15,000 each. Volunteers from Community Faith Partners and organizations such as Smith Heating Plumbing & Electrical, Bethel Grove Bible Church and 84 Lumber have helped erect the cottages. Private donations fund the construction and residents (all men) pay rent as they are able.

Carmen formed Second Wind Cottages and donated 7 acres of property to the nonprofit. There were no zoning issues. The city simply asked them to submit some plans for the site and buildings. The problem arose when men started living in the houses. A few of the residents were sexual offenders. Carmen knew from attending the area Continuum of Care (CoC) meetings that no other homeless provider would house them. When the neighbors discovered that Carmen had men convicted of sex crimes living at Second Wind, they organized to expel the homeless men from Newfield. Carmen attended several community meetings, presenting his position. He strongly asserted that the ex-convicts had served their time and deserved a second chance. He indicated that about half of the town has been converted and is supportive of the village.

Motivated by his faith, Carmen instinctively used the "Housing First" model without knowing there was a name for what he was doing. He had and has reservations about programs that have rules concerning sobriety or medication compliance. He describes his philosophy as "walking with people on their journey." Social workers tend to talk about "meeting people where they are." Some of the residents have been at Second Wind for

SECOND WIND Above: The neat and identical "cottages" are lined up in a row. Below: Each house has electricity and plumbing, furnishings and appliances. Photos provided by Second Wind and used with permission.

four years. After they finish constructing all 19 cottages, Carmen hopes to add a community building and to replicate the residential project for women and children in a separate location.

The mayor of Ithaca has offered high praise for the impromptu development. In fact, the city has secured some rent money for the village's tenants. When asked about other shelter options Richard Bennett, director of the Ithaca Rescue Mission, explained to a reporter that there aren't an adequate number of beds because Ithaca is the eighth most expensive place to live in the United States and that it has a vacancy rate of only 0.5 percent. Residents can remain at Second Wind indefinitely.[26] There is a waiting list for new applicants. (Unfortunately, The Jungle didn't remain unoccupied. There are actually three sections of The Jungle, two that belong to the city and the third is property of the railroad. Despite his developments, Carmen still visits The Jungle.)

Community First! Village in East Austin, Texas (2015-present)

As with Second Wind, Community First! Village has religious roots. Alan Graham owned a lucrative real estate business in his 20s.[27] It provided a comfortable suburban life for him, his wife and their four children. In his mid-30s, Alan returned to the Roman Catholic Church and, at 41, he was talked into attending a spiritual life retreat with other men from St. John Neumann's Parish. The event changed him so much so that he volunteered to lead a second retreat.

It was during the later retreat that Alan had a vision of incorporating trucks into a feeding program for homeless people in Austin. He quickly recruited some other men including Houston Flake, who had been homeless and was working as the custodian of Alan's church, to start Mobile Loaves & Fishes. Then, in September 1998, they began distributing sack lunches downtown Austin. By December, Alan and his friends had raised $25,000—enough to buy a used Ford pickup truck. They custom-built a catering station and fit it into the truck's bed. The catering truck design allows people living on the street to select what food items they wanted rather than merely taking a meal that has been predetermined. Today, according to their website, the nonprofit runs six trucks, seven days a week in Austin and San Antonio, Texas; Providence, Rhode Island; and Minneapolis, Minnesota utilizing 19,000 volunteers.

Mobile Loaves & Fishes purchased a gently used RV to shelter one of the men who frequented its food truck. That sparked the idea of creating an RV park for people who were living on the streets. Initially, Alan tried to create the park in Austin. His idea garnered the support of the mayor but public resistance aborted the project. Then a 27-acre parcel sitting just outside Austin's boundary was identified. Alan convinced the city to extend the water lines to the property so the campus could be hooked up for plumbing. Thus, Community First! Village took more than one year to start.

Soon, people began giving the village campers. Today, 100 refurbished RVs are available for people who have been homeless. There are also 12-by-12 canvas-sided cottages and 121 to 180 square feet tiny houses. The tent cottages are helpful for individuals who need to become accustomed to living indoors once more. Area architects designed a number of the tiny house structures so that they have interesting features like a second story deck. A few of the houses were purchased from an outfit in Astonia. These houses cost $5,500 to purchase and end up with a price tag of roughly $20,000 for the finished product if they are assembled by local churches. All of the buildings have electricity while the bathhouses, kitchens and laundry facilities are communal. The quality of the buildings is outstanding.

The village includes a number of activities. Many of them provide jobs for the residents. For instance, some people work in the blacksmith program, creating a variety of products out of metal. Others assist a carpenter at the woodworking shop or paint art pieces in the studio. Still more are engaged with outsiders who oversee a large community garden. Six residents handle housekeeping at the Airbnb hotel. A few are employed in the maintenance building where the RV campers are made ready for service. Still, there is a rural and rustic feel to the property on

Community First! Above: These tiny houses and campers in the front of the village are actually used as an Airbnb (hotel) but it is representative of the mix of units in Community First!—tiny houses, tents and RV campers. There are also four oversized teepees that are part of the hotel. Below: This is one of several community kitchens that are partially covered by a building and partially exposed to the elements. All of the equipment is commercial-grade.

Hog Eye Road. A huge chicken coop provides eggs for break-fasts and a beehive supplies fresh honey. Milk and cheese come from resident goats and the village supports a catfish farm.

Individuals wanting to live at Community First! must complete the coordinated assessment process, provide fingerprints for an FBI check and criminal background check.[28] They must also provide proof of homelessness for at least a year within the Austin metropolitan area. This determines whether a person is qualified. The village targets chronically homeless people who have a high utilization of crisis services—hospitals, psychiatric facilities, jails, etc. Residents pay rent. The amount is determined by the style of housing they occupy. The cheapest monthly fee is $50 for a canvas-sided cottage. The most expensive monthly rent is $360 for a tiny house. The tiny homes are for single individuals while the RVs accommodate families. Residents are allowed to own one pet.

Approximately 20 "missional" folks live in the village, too. Everyone can stay indefinitely. In fact, there is a medical clinic, and hospice care is available. There is even a memorial garden named after Larry "Taz" Williams," a homeless man who played an integral part in establishing Community First! On the day I visited, Jim, the assistant chaplain, announced that another Jim, a member of the village, had died downtown that day. Ironically, someone from the Scott Building at Cass had died the same day, too. What a comfort to the community members to know that there is a final resting place at the village where loved ones can visit.

Visitors have unfettered access to the campus. The village perimeter is outlined with a walking trail. You won't find Alan Graham exercising on it, though. He is busy fundraising for a large sanctuary building and the second phase of the village. The organization has purchased 24 acres next door, which will house 350 additional people.

The Cottages at Hickory Crossing in Dallas, Texas (2016-present)

The leadership of the Central Dallas Community Development Corporation (Central Dallas CDC) began considering the potential of using the tiny detached houses that were developed for the Gulf States following Hurricane Katrina as a solution to homelessness in Texas. The Katrina Cottages were quick and inexpensive to construct and relatively easy to maintain. The distinctive design was also architecturally attractive. In 2009, when the W.W. Caruth Jr. Foundation brought together six key community agencies to address the growing tent city population, the recommendation to use the cottages was adopted.[29]

Fundraising for the 50 400-square-foot houses required five years and resulted in the $6.8 million needed to cover the budget. The cottages were financed through a public/private partnership between the Dallas County Criminal Justice Department, University of Texas Southwestern Medical Center, Metrocare Services, Central Dallas CDC and a number of private donors including the Highland Park United Methodist Church and the Preston Hollow Presbyterian Church Foundation. Highland Park UMC contributed $100,000 for two houses and Preston Hollow PCF provided funding for another house.

Property was identified near the intersection of Macolm X Boulevard and I-30. It is steps away from a bus line which transports passengers to downtown Dallas. It is also directly across the street from CitySquare's Opportunity Center, which houses programs for food distribution, vocational training and a myriad of other social services. The nonprofits broke ground for Hickory Crossing late in 2014. Central Dallas CDC served as the developer for the project.

Hickory Crossing operates a Housing First program for 50 chronically homeless individuals. Residents were chosen from a list of 300 individuals using data from Parkland Health & Hospital System and Dallas County Jail. The idea was to identify people who had used the most public services, were the most expensive to taxpayers, and to provide them permanent housing.

HICKORY CROSSING Above: Unfortunately no one could give me permission to take photos of the cottages inside the village on the days I was there. It is an extremely beautiful campus with stunning landscaping. Even this side view shows the warm exterior colors and the quality of the construction. The photo also provides a glimpse of the proximity of the cottages to the highway. What is missing from the shot is the Dallas skyline that is visible from the village. Below: On Martin Luther King Jr. Blvd., just blocks from Hickory Crossing, are encampments under the highway bridges. The tents are the dark shadows in the background of the picture. The trash is piled up because on the day I was there, they were cleaning up the area.

CitySquare's Larry James estimates that the housing at Hickory Crossing will save the county $25,000 per person annually.[30] A small group moved into the houses initially, then two adults at a time occupied units in a staggered schedule until the complex was full in the spring of 2017.

Since every resident of Hickory Crossing has a mental health diagnosis and several have been incarcerated, most benefit from a wide range of services. In addition to the ones available at Opportunity Center, many services are conveniently offered on-site including medical and mental health care through Metrocare Services. Two connected buildings make up the entrance of the village. The floor-to-ceiling glass facilities accommodate a laundry room and 3,000 square feet of office and meeting spaces. The village utilizes a collaborative team approach so that there is a 6:1 ratio of residents to staff members. A small number of volunteers augment the employees. For instance, an outside volunteer staffs the receptionist area.

Nickelsville Union Tiny House Village in Seattle, Washington (2016-present)

In 2015, more than 45 people died on the streets of Seattle, Washington and in November of that year, Mayor Ed Murray declared a homelessness state of emergency. One of Seattle's strategies to combat the growing number of at-risk, unhoused people was to sanction encampments within the city's bounds and to provide funding for them.[31]

Prior to that, in 2014, Pastor Steve Olsen had leased undeveloped land about a mile away from downtown Seattle and established a camp with his associate, Scott Morrow, called Nickelsville. The name Nickelsville was chosen as a way to protest the anti-encampments policies of Seattle's former mayor, Greg Nickels. There was a period of tumultuous history in 2015 and the homeless people were ultimately evicted in March of 2016.

Also in 2016, Nickelsville and Olsen's Lutheran Church of the Good Shepherd joined together with the Low Income Housing Institute to open a 14 tiny house village on the church's property, just doors down the block on East Union Street. A single-family home formerly occupied the parcel, so the 96-square-foot houses are arranged close together. They form a circle with a central building that supplies the village's bathrooms (flush toilets, sinks, a shower with hot and cold water). There is also a community kitchen. The tiny houses have electricity and space heaters but few amenities. They were donated and Environmental Works, a nonprofit Community Design Center, was instrumental in planning and designing the unique site.

Housing in Nicklesville Union is considered transitional and residents tend to stay about six months. They pay $90 a month to cover their utilities. The village can accommodate singles, couples and families. The houses cost approximately $2,200 each and are intended to shelter two people. In addition to opening Union, Nickelsville started adding tiny houses to its Othello and Ballard camps.

NICKELSVILLE: Left: Nickelsville Union occupies a single lot in close proximity to Good Shepherd Lutheran Church.
Above: Nickelsville Ballard has five new tiny houses built and decorated by the Tulalip Tribe. Other houses have been donated by Sawhorse Revolution and Youthbuild.
Below: Nickelsvillle Ballard contains tents as well as the tiny houses that hug the fence.

Notes for the Snapshot of Programs Utilizing Tiny Houses (on pages 52-53):
*   Nickelsville Union is only one of the nonprofit's growing number of locations.
**   Construction costs for Quixote are listed in some sources as $89,000 and others as $102,000. As with all of the costs listed, it varies on what is included as construction. Some tiny house village divide their total construction costs (land, architectural services, environmental inspections, labor costs, material costs, etc.) to determine unit costs. Others include far fewer things and, so, the snapshot provides a general idea of the money required vs. actual expenses.*

A Snapshot of Program

	Dignity Village	Opportunity Village	Quixote Village	Occupy Madison
City, State	Portland, OR	Eugene, OR	Olympia, WA	Madison, WI
Year	2004	2013	2013	2014
Non-Profit	Dignity Village, Inc.	SquareOne Village	Panza	Occupy Madison Inc.
Square Footage	120 sf	60-80 sf	144 sf	98 sf
# of Units	43	29 (Not all TH)	30	9
Foundations	Pier Blocks	Pier Blocks	Poured Piers	Trailer-beds
Builders	Residents and Volunteers	Residents and Volunteers	Contractor	Residents and Volunteers
Construction Unit Costs	$3,000	$2,400	$102,000**	$4,000
Land Ownership/Cost	City Owned	City Owned	Thurston County	Nonprofit- $110,000
Electricity	Common Bldgs	Common Bldgs	Each Unit	Trailer Hook-up
Sanitation	4 Common Port-a-potties and 1 Shower	2 Bathrooms and 1 Shower in Common Bath House	1/2 baths in Units and shared Toilets/Showers in Common Bldg	3 Bathrooms and 2 Showers Common Bldg
Kitchen	Outside Cooking	Outside Cooking	Common Bldg	Common Bldg
HVAC	Propane Tanks (residents pay to refill)	Heat only in Yurt and Bath House	Heat in Units and Common Bldg	Heat in Units an Common Bldg
Resident Fees	$35 plus $10 a month plus 10 hrs of labor a week	$30 a month plus 10 hours of labor per week	30% of Income	32 hours to mov in and 10 hour weekly until 53
Type of Housing	Transitional	Transitional	Permanent Supportive	Permanent
Governance	Self-Governance	Village Council & Nonprofit Board	Resident Council & Nonprofit Board	2 Residents or Nonprofit Boar
Zoning	Transitional Campground	Homeless Shelter	Permanent Homeless Encampment	Commercial
Web Site	dignityvillage.org	squareonevillages. org/opportunity	quixotevillage.com	occupymadiso inc.com

Utilizing Tiny Houses

Second Wind	Community First!	Hickory Crossing	Nickelsville Union*	Cass Tiny Homes
Newfield, NY	East Austin, TX	Dallas, TX	Seattle, WA	Detroit, MI
2014	2015	2016	2016	2016
Second Wind Cottages	Mobile Loaves & Fishes	CitySquare	LIHI & Nickelsville	Cass Community Social Services, Inc.
320 sf	121-300 sf	400 sf	96 sf	250-400 sf
19	250 (Not all TH)	50	14	25
Slab on Grade	Various	Poured Piers	Pier Blocks	Slab on Grade
All Volunteers	Volunteers and Contractor	Contractor	Volunteers	Contractor and Volunteers
$15,000	$30,000	$50,000	$2,200	$45,000-$65,000
Nonprofit- donated from Auto Shop $115,000	Nonprofit- $16,000,000	Nonprofit- $750,000	Lutheran Church of the Good Shepherd	Nonprofit- $15,000
Each Unit	Various	Each Unit	Each Unit	Each Unit
Toilet, Sink and Shower in Each Home	Communal Restrooms and Showers	Toilet, Sink and Shower in Each Unit	2 Toilets/1 Shower in Detached Restroom	Toilet, Sink and Shower/Tub in Each Home
Each Unit	Common Bldgs	Each Unit	Kitchen Tent	Each Unit
Heat in Each Unit	Space heaters in units. AC by request	Each Unit	Space Heaters	Heat & AC PTAC in Each Home
25% of income as able	$225 -$360 per month	30% of income	$90 a month	$250-$400/month for 7 years
Transitional	Permanent Supportive	Permanent Supportive	Transitional	Home Ownership
NA	NA	NA	LIHI Financial/ Nickelsville Operations	Resident Council then Home Owners Association
Commercial	No zoning in Texas	No zoning in Texas	Transitional Encampment	Residential
secondwind cottages.org	mlf.org	citysquare.org	lihi.org/tiny-houses	casscommunity. org

Jade ▓▓▓ Imagine that, real solutions for real problems for humanity. Humanity. Solutions
Like · Reply · September 13, 2016 at 11:42pm
Wayne ▓▓▓ Good idea for the working poor.
Like · Reply · September 13, 2016 at 11:47pm
Gaby ▓▓▓ This house is normal size in the Netherlands.
Like · Reply · September 14, 2016 at 12:55am
Debbie ▓▓▓ Why is this different from a mobile home park ???
Like · Reply · September 16, 2016 at 7:17pm
Drena ▓▓▓ Waste of good money. . Invest in the homes that need rehab.. before you want build another. That are get communities/homes that once where neglected now are worth 225,000 just to rehab. We, have grand old brick, Victorian, Flank Lloyd Wright, Colonial and style home it represents in Detroit. .
Like · Reply · September 16, 2016 at 7:17pm
Debbie ▓▓▓ They are gorgeous. #
Like · Reply · September 16, 2016 at 7:17pm
Mette ▓▓▓ The sizes are similar to Danish homes, nice and comfy. 😊 Bigger isn't always better.
Like · Reply · September 17, 2016 at 5:39am
Kyle ▓▓▓ This is a long shot........ Detroit isn't like Austin and Portland. Get a clue.
Like · Reply · September 19, 2016 at 9:00am
Ernest ▓▓▓ That's like an average size house in UK 😄
Like · Reply · September 24, 2016 at 4:04am

4

Not a Village

I GREW UP on the east side of Detroit. My parents moved
our family of six from an upstairs flat on Lenox Street to a
single-family home on Jane Street, not too far from the City
Airport (today called the Coleman A. Young Municipal Airport). Buying a house was important to my parents because it
meant that they could put down roots. For my brothers and me,
it meant we could have a dog. The house sat 25 feet or so off
the sidewalk on a deep, 37-by-168-foot lot with a garage that
hugged the alley where we burned fall leaves and cooked apples
from the old tree in the backyard.

Ours was part of a middle-class neighborhood that was close-
knit. Fifty years later, I still recollect most of the people by name.
Next door, there was an elderly couple, the Knapps, who owned
a scrappy sheepdog. Their middle-aged daughter, Millie, checked
in on them a couple of times each week. My mother referred to
her as a "spinster." The Knapps would argue with each other in
the backyard and Mr. Knapp would routinely yell at us from the
front porch to stay off their lawn while we were riding our bikes.

On the other side of our three-bedroom house lived Frances Perguno, a kind widow. Her son Tony and his wife stayed upstairs. Frances would offer me Italian treats and she allowed my mother to cut lilacs off the bush that grew along her fence. We would display them in a clear pop bottle or jelly jar inside our house as if they had come from a florist. The fragrance was always amazing.

Beside Frances' duplex, a senior citizen named Oli lived with her grandson Gillard in what today would be called a tiny house. It sat way back on the deep lot as if it had once been a garage. My older brothers played with Gillard but I was never included. Oli came from Belgium. Her family received food from the United States during World War I thanks to Warren Harding.

Across the street, there was a corner market—Randazzo's. They had fresh meat and produce that the owner, Andy, bought from Eastern Market. He made his own Italian sausage. On Sundays, the market also sold doughnuts, rolls, cannolis and little round pizzas delivered from Tringali's Bakery. I remember that the door to Andy and Ann's apartment was tucked in behind the meat counter.

The Thorntons lived next to the store—Marble and Russ with their children Randy and Candi. An older daughter Judy was married and lived with her husband some blocks away. The thing about Judy was that she and her brother Jimmy both contracted polio. Jimmy died and Judy spent nine months in an iron lung at Herman Kiefer Hospital. She survived, but her arms were permanently paralyzed. From age 15, Judy used her mouth and toes to accomplish everything: picking up papers, dialing a telephone and using utensils for eating. Grandma Thornton lived in an apartment upstairs.

Next to the Thorntons, directly across from our house, lived the DeLorenzos, a devoted Roman Catholic family. Rudy and Joyce were the parents of Rudy and Lydia. I remember that Rudy Sr. approached my father to ask whether he thought Bishop Gallagher would be a good high school for his son. My dad was a public school teacher but he was the product of a Catholic education. He graduated from St. Ambrose and the

University of Detroit. Like so many houses on our block, the DeLorenzo's included an aunt and an uncle, Nina and Pio, who resided with them. The uncle had escaped the Fascists in Italy.

We associated with people further down the block, too. The Rose family had five children, several of whom matched my siblings and me age-wise. While playing with Ronnie Rose one day before starting school, I smashed an Etch A Sketch over his head because he wouldn't let me play with the aluminum powder art board. My parents were not amused. Wayne Rose owned a gas station and auto repair shop on Chalmers. When his wife, Liz, learned that my father was part Native American, she wanted him to wear his headdress down to their house so everyone could see it.

Then there were the Klines. Pauline and Phil had a talented daughter, Betty Jean, who played the violin and rode with my dad to work. He taught at Commerce High School at the time and she attended Cass Tech (a high school that attracted the brightest and best students from across the city). The two high schools were connected by a skywalk until Commerce was razed to accommodate the I-75 expressway. The Klines used to ask the Fowler children over periodically to listen to us play our musical instruments. We were horrible, but they never let on.

Marge and Chick Chandler's house was at that end of the block. Several times they paid me to walk their big Boxer while they were out of town. A Polish couple lived near them. Both husband and wife had thick accents, so it was difficult to understand what they were saying. At the very end of Jane Street, a single mother raised two children. The little boy was a hemophiliac. We were afraid to play with him because we were sure that he would get hurt somehow and bleed to death. No one wanted to be held responsible for that.

The Ritter Bowling Alley was located on the opposite corner. Inside the 11,000-square-foot brick building there were 12 wooden lanes, pinball machines and a pizzeria. They even had an in-house pro named Paul Cito. Ritter's had the only air conditioning on either side of the block. I recall that they had a sign in the door window that said, "Come inside where it is Kool," advertising the cigarettes that they sold from a machine and the fact that on hot days it was comfortable in the bowling alley.

All of this is to say that although Andrew Heben's book, *Tent City Urbanism*, is insightful—crammed full of architectural history and planning research, encampment observations and village suggestions—I am not convinced that the grid pattern is bad for community building. I grew up on a rectangular block where we interacted with our neighbors. We didn't have a village square on Jane Street. People sat on their porches—their front porches as well as the back ones. Children played pickle on the sidewalks and touch football in the street. They rode bikes together. Parents pushed strollers and walked their dogs up and down the block. We walked each other's dogs. Neighbors invited children to perform in their living rooms as if they belonged to the von Trapp family.

Although our house never had air conditioning like the bowling alley, I can recall when we got a color television set. I think it was 19 inches. It may have been smaller. It certainly didn't have a flat screen; nor was it outfitted with a Bose surround sound system. There wasn't any cable with which to connect and so, as with our black-and-white model, we balled up aluminum foil and placed it on the tops of the two antennae that protruded upward like *My Favorite Martian*. It was well before VCRs and Blockbuster. No one was binge-watching shows from Netflix. There were just three networks and, because Canada was just across the river, we got additional shows from Windsor. Remote control? LOL! I'm convinced that children were conceived back in the day just to jump up and change the channel. My parents put the color TV on a snack table on the front porch and a good number of the neighbors brought their folding chairs over and set them up on the lawn. People shared. We had a magnificent community.

In fact, I would assert that poor people, including people who have been homeless, may do better blending into an existing neighborhood. There is a stigma when folks are segregated. The view-obscuring fences and single point of entry design of most tiny house villages may be helpful in limiting access but it also sends the message that the population must be controlled and that the neighborhood prefers them to be out of sight. The Tiny Homes at Cass were created to be integrated into the neighborhood, in fact, to help resurrect the area.

Each home sits on its own lot like every other house. Most parcels are 30 feet by 100 feet. The homes face the street and have both front and back yards. All of them include a front porch or a back deck/patio. They have all of the amenities of their neighbors—indoor plumbing, heat and air conditioning, a stove and refrigerator, a washer and dryer, and every house has its own security system. That is where the conformity stops. No two houses are identical. Each is attractive and distinctive—with details and features as different as the people who reside in them.

Cass' development does not use the village model. Moreover, it is not the outgrowth of a protest against shelter conditions or the criminalization of homelessness or the 1 percent (Occupy Movement). Cass Community Social Services is a social services provider. We operate emergency housing programs: a warming center for women and children; a rotating shelter in conjunction with area churches; a family shelter; as well as a number of permanent supportive housing programs.

We know that shelters and, to a lesser degree residential programs, are not perfect. Not ours. Not those who tout "best practices." Compiling the list below of "Why You Should Avoid Spending Time in a Shelter" is a relatively easy task:

1. **Beds are limited.** If the shelter is crowded you may end up sleeping on an air mattress or on the floor—or you may not even be admitted at all. Depending on the city, shelter space may be less than 50 percent or even as low as 25 percent of the homeless population.

2. **Shelters are understaffed.** Grants barely cover the basic operational costs of meals, utilities, cleaning supplies, etc. Since these things are required, agencies tend to balance their budgets by skimping on the number of staff available.

3. **Storage space for possessions is at a premium.** What you can't securely store may be stolen or broken.

(See #2) Because unhoused people have only a few things, losing just one of them can be traumatic. If the item is something critical like shoes or a government-issued cell phone, theft involves a tremendous setback. (Other critical possessions of people experiencing homelessness include items such as birth certificates, social security cards, photo identification, family photos and medication.) Most homeless people aren't robbers but the few who are cause serious hardship.

4. **You may be barred.** If you steal or are violent, you may not be admitted. (Extreme violence usually means that you are permanently banned.)

5. **You may be separated from your family members.** Heterosexual or homosexual couples are routinely split up and teenage boys may be forced to stay in a men's shelter because sleeping areas are set up like congregate barracks. Single fathers rarely have shelter options for keeping their families intact.

6. **You parent in public.** This can be taxing for both the adult and the children. There is very little privacy in most shelters for anything.

7. **Many discriminate against or aren't able to accommodate LGBTQ adults or teens.** Since the majority of shelters are gender-specific, LGBTQ (lesbian, gay, bisexual, transgender, queer/questioning) individuals are sometimes denied services.

8. **Most won't allow you to have an animal.** Many homeless people keep pets for companionship and/or for protection. Some shelters won't even allow a guide dog. (Note: in large groups, there is bound to be someone who is afraid of dogs or allergic to dogs or cats.)

9. **You may be hurt.** Occasionally people become violent in shelters. Also, predators sometimes target individuals leaving/arriving at the building for robbery or rape. This includes children and youth.

10. **You may be disrespected.** It may be by a staff member, volunteer or another person staying in the shelter. This could be the result of someone making judgments about you or how you became homeless. Many people feel disrespected by having to answer intake or case management questions that can be invasive.

11. **You may contract a disease.** Imagine how an outbreak of the flu sweeps through a shelter with common bathrooms and sleeping quarters. It is not unusual for people living on the streets to have life-threatening and contagious diseases like tuberculosis or hepatitis.

12. **The shelter staff or volunteers may try to proselytize you.** This may happen even though you are of another faith, or are agnostic or atheist. A minority of shelters require unhoused people to pray, attend services and/or make a confession of faith before eating or sleeping inside.

13. **The hours of operation may jeopardize your job or schooling.** Shelters tend to open in the afternoon and close during the daytime. If your work or school schedule causes you to come in after curfew, some expel you. If you work night shifts, you won't be able to sleep during the day. If it is raining or snowing, boiling or freezing outside, a weekend or a holiday, most require you to leave during the day. Because shelters have limited capacity, many have people stand in line until the doors open. This procedure can be incompatible with the normal 9-to-5 workday, as well.

14. **You may lose control.** Someone else decides when and what institutional food you will eat; when you go to bed and when you get up; if you can use the phone or laundry; when you can watch TV and what you watch. Someone else controls the thermostat. Do you

have trouble sleeping with lights on? The fire marshal determines what emergency lights must remain lit.

15. **It is loud.** At night you may not be able to fall asleep because colicky babies cry, sick people hack and people with mental illnesses sometimes talk to themselves. Individuals who are self-medicating frequently yell and/or use obscenities even in the presence of children. (If not monitored, behaviors and television shows/movies may not be age-appropriate for children to watch either.)

16. **It isn't comfortable.** You sit on a bed or a folding chair. None of the beds have pillow tops or high thread-count sheets. There are no La-Z-Boy recliners or cushy couches. Many bathrooms are equipped with seatless, stainless steel prison-style toilets and, because people both steal the toilet paper and flush entire rolls down the commodes, it is doled out on an as-needed basis.

17. **There are bugs.** No matter how clean a building is or what precautions the exterminator takes, shelters are highly susceptible to parasites as people habitually bring in bed bugs, scabies and lice. Squirreling away food in the shelter can also infest the area with cockroaches, gnats, flies and mice.

18. **There are community restrooms and shower stalls.**

19. **A few people won't wash up.** Often, the stench of urine and body odors will permeate the air. Think of breathing the smell of dirty diapers that are as potent as nail polish remover. The thing that reeks the worst, I have found, are feet that have only one pair of well-worn sneakers, especially wet shoes.

20. **Your past may make it difficult.** Anyone who has been incarcerated will find it troublesome to submit to searches of their bags and/or bodies and veterans will dislike being cooped up inside.

To be fair, the majority of shelters and residential programs for homeless people are operated by staff members who are kind and caring. They are attracted to social work because they want to make a difference and want to help others. Many nonprofits, like ours, employ individuals who have been homeless and/or have struggled with addiction and/or mental illness. They work with unhoused people to implement policies and procedures that optimize safety, confidentiality, dignity and support. My observation is that the "better" agencies are consistently at or over capacity. In the final analysis, few facilities would score poorly on all of the items on the above list and, in fact, a good number of organizations would certainly receive excellent scores.

The truth is that it is harrowing to be homeless. If *The Grapes of Wrath* raised awareness of what people endured living in a tent city, reading or watching the movie *The Pursuit of Happyness* can drive home how quickly someone can become homeless and what a challenge it is to turn things around afterward.[32] Actor Will Smith plays real-life Chris Gardner. Gardner was living in San Francisco, a wonderful, hilly city on the bay that has extremely expensive housing. Gardner invested all of his money in bone-density scanners with the goal of selling them to area doctors as a superior alternative to X-rays. In fact, he was a persuasive sales person but his pitch often fell on deaf ears as he tried to unload the last several machines.

The middle part of the story seems almost too good and too bad to be true. Gardner met a manager for Dean Witter Reynolds. The two of them shared a taxi and, during the ride, Gardner amazed the businessman by pivoting and twisting the six colors of a Rubik's Cube until the each face was solved. The meeting would result in Gardner winning an unpaid internship that could lead to a six-figure broker position. Unfortunately, before he went to the interview, Chris was forced to run away from the cab driver because he didn't have fare money. In the process, he lost one of his expensive scanners. The financial pressure eroded his marriage.

The unpaid position was the last straw for his wife, who had been working as a motel maid. She left Gardner and their

5-year-old son, Christopher Jr., hoping to secure better employment in New York. Then, his bank account was garnished for back taxes. The father and son were evicted. They were homeless with $22 between them. Part of the reason I was drawn to the story is that I knew that Gardner had received services at Glide, a church and nonprofit similar to Cass in San Francisco. The movie showed the duo moving between their homeless shelter, a hotel and a BART station. The overnight episode in the BART bathroom, where Gardner jammed the door with his legs is gut-wrenching. All the pieces of his life had come crashing down like dominos colliding into one another until he was physically prone on a public bathroom floor expending his last ounce of strength, using his body to protect the only thing he had left, his son.

No, shelters are not perfect, and yet in places like Detroit, the majority of people experiencing homelessness use the shelter system. Coming inside defends them from hypothermia during the winters. (Ours and others, by the way, do not put people out during the daytime hours.) Shelters provide them with meals that are prepared in kitchens that are regularly inspected. Individuals staying in a shelter have access to indoor plumbing: restrooms, showers, laundry services. Shelters generally distribute toilet paper, feminine hygiene supplies, soap, shampoo, conditioner, hand lotion, deodorant, diapers and formula for babies. Clean and dry clothing, coats, and sometimes shoes and boots, are made available to folks. The conditions may be crowded but there is usually a bed with clean sheets and a pillow. Most shelters give people access to a telephone, television, the Internet and electricity for their own devices. What's more, shelters and warming centers today act as a front door to other services, including permanent housing.

Women and men complete an assessment when they first come inside during what is called the "intake process." In Detroit, an intake staff member administers the VI-SPDAT (vulnerability index-service prioritization decision assistance tool). The questionnaire scores individuals in terms of their risk and prioritization. Their needs are aligned with resources based on their VI-SPDAT score: The people who can probably solve their own issues are rated for no housing support, others with mid-level needs are ranked for rapid re-housing and adults who have the greatest vulnerabilities, as indicated by the highest scores, are slated for permanent supportive housing. Then, a SPDAT is administered by CAM (Coordinated Assessment Model) staff members to ensure that the middle and highest scores were accurate. They are then placed on the appropriate waiting list. Those with the highest scores are at the top of the list.

Chronically and literally homeless people are then eligible for supportive housing which could subsidize their housing indefinitely and provide case management to help them stay successfully housed. The problem with this program is that while the system places the most in need with housing first, those who have not been homeless as long or do not have a disability are pushed further down the list as those with higher needs come into the system. Therefore, many individuals remain homeless and without a definitive timeframe for receiving housing.

Moderately scored applicants are assigned to rapid re-housing which means that they would receive funds to pay a security deposit and first month's rent as well as a subsidy to cover three months to two years rent. Here, too, the need far exceeds the supply. Therefore, waiting lists are long. There is not a timeframe. Furthermore, once a person is housed, the subsidy is time-limited so if the renter fails to secure adequate income within the subsidy period, his/her housing is jeopardized once again.

To recap, some individuals do not qualify for housing assistance and those who do generally have an extended wait due to the lack of affordable housing and the limited number of subsidies. Thus, shelter and residential programs for people experiencing homelessness are unable to turn over beds for new people because those ready to leave (individuals who have identification, a source of income, are clean and sober, etc.) have nowhere to go.

Unlike the village model, which seeks to offer Housing First for individuals, Cass Tiny Homes is intended for people who are ready to leave the shelters or residential programs. The villages have a goal of getting people off the streets and out of tent cities, while the Cass objective is to move them out of the shelters/residential programs so that beds will be freed up for people still living outside; and to assist those who have aspirations of establishing wealth. Put another way, the village approach puts an emphasis on ending homelessness and creating community. The tiny homes at Cass have the goal of ending poverty and integrating people into an existing city neighborhood.

The Ritter Bowling alley at the end of my childhood street is still standing but has a new owner.

Above: The house on Jane Street where I grew up is no longer there. Nor are the houses that stood behind it on the other side of the alley and several blocks down. On the right of the lot where my house stood is a boarded up Habitat House and to the left is an occupied Habitat House. Below: My best friend Julie's house on Flanders Street, the other side of Jane. Today it stands completely open to the elements and the garage floor is covered with illegally dumped tires.

Laureen ▮▮▮▮ 10,000 dollars worth of building materials is all it takes to build small house like that. If they go to restore for doors and windows and fixtures it could be less
Like · Reply · September 19, 2016 at 12:52pm

Christine ▮▮▮▮ Like habitat for humanity. They help build their home then 95% don't pay their pay their bills and run the new house into the ground.
Like · Reply · September 17, 2016 at 4:58am

5

Home Ownership

UNLIKE NEW YORK or Chicago (with their acres of apartment buildings), Detroit has had a history of single-family homes.[33] In the late 1800s, they were Victorian homes built with turrets and leaded glass like the Whitney on Woodward Avenue and Canfield, built by lumber baron David Whitney for his wife; or the smaller worker's cottages in the Corktown neighborhood. From about 1910 to the 1930s, several one and a half story bungalows, many of them craftsmen-style homes, were erected as were a lesser number of two-story flats both wood and brick. Owners lived on the first floors, and their tenants or renters stayed upstairs on streets like Rosa Parks Boulevard (formerly 12th Street).

After World War II, as families grew, the bungalows were made typically larger with two bedrooms, a bathroom and an unfinished attic. These new houses finished filling out the city and started spilling into the suburbs like Oak Park and East Detroit, Livonia and Roseville. They measured 800 to 1,000 square feet and cost an average of $9,750. Brick ranch-style homes were becoming popular during that period.

By the mid-'50s, new houses had 1,300 square feet with three bedrooms and a bath and a half. Forced-air heating units allowed for compact furnaces and additional space in the basements for recreational activities such as pool or ping pong, play areas for the children and family rooms. Exhaust fans and garbage disposals became standard with these houses, which became prominent in the suburban neighborhoods. They went up by the thousands in places like Pontiac, Clawson, Madison Heights, Royal Oak, Birmingham, Lincoln Park, Allen Park and Taylor. The average cost climbed to $13,000.

When the baby boomers reached their 20s, in the '70s and '80s, they started purchasing houses and spurred construction in the out-county areas. Subdivisions featured 1,650- to 2,000-square-foot, two-story colonials with attached garages. During the '90s, real estate classified ads began appearing for 3,000-square-foot houses listed at prices of $400,000 or more. In 2000, 73 huge houses in Oakland County went on the market for a million dollars and up.

Metropolitan Detroit has been distinguished for a century by single-family homes. Thus, founding a local Habitat for Humanity made perfect sense. The Christian nonprofit began providing affordable housing for low- to moderate-income individuals and families in Detroit in 1986.[34] In 1993, Habitat established its headquarters and a workshop in the old Ritter Bowling Alley at the end of my childhood street, Jane. Initially it renovated properties, but Habitat for Humanity Detroit went on to put up 100 houses in the first 16 years, including the Oprah Winfrey house in the Creekside neighborhood. In 2005, former President Jimmy Carter joined Detroit's Blitz Build work project in June, gathering 1,500 volunteers to build 30 houses in one week and garnering international press coverage.

In 2008, they began building ENERGY STAR certified houses. Volunteer crews employed Greenbuild construction techniques to lessen the negative impact on the environment in terms of building materials: windows, insulation, etc. ENERGY STAR appliances were also installed. By the time they celebrated their 25th anniversary in 2012, the Detroit chapter had also opened two Habitat ReStore facilities, one on the east side of the city and the other on the west side. In January of 2016, Kenneth Cockrel Jr., former city council president and former mayor, was recruited to be the CEO of Habitat for Humanity Detroit.

Unfortunately, in January 2017 after a year of networking and fundraising, Cockrel announced that Habitat for Humanity Detroit would need to restructure its operations.[35] It laid off most its employees and closed both ReStore locations. He explained the actions were necessary because the ReStores had not been profitable, coupled with a loss of government funding and less income from corporate sponsorships. He also stated that when he joined the organization, it had a mortgage delinquency rate over of 40 percent among homeowners and a large number of empty homes.

The news was as devastating for Detroit as it was for Habitat in that the organization had provided the possibility of homeownership and wealth-building to people who had historically had been denied both. Three hundred years of slavery meant that African-Americans were property and couldn't own land much less pass it on to their heirs. Federal policies since the New Deal favored new construction in white suburban areas and discouraged investment in the city, particularly in integrated neighborhoods. For decades, real estate agents blatantly practiced redlining with federal policies to back them up. Add to that, the guidelines that excluded agricultural workers and domestic help from the social security system. Finally, Aid to Families with Dependent Children (AFDC) restricted poor families from developing assets from 1994 to 2004.

The news was dismal because Habitat stood in stark contrast to financial institutions whose practices contributed to the subprime loan crisis. Habitat utilized traditional ways of verifying credit worthiness. They avoided "affordable" mortgage products, which featured low down payments, higher debt burdens and minimal cash reserves. They didn't entice poor people to sign-up for the interest-only, adjustable interest rates, balloon payments or pre-payment penalty mortgages, which had a high probability of ending in foreclosure and triggering the decline of the housing stock in an entire neighborhood. From 1994 to 2004, subprime loans increased 15-fold and the odds of foreclosure were undeniably linked to race and place.[36] As a nonprofit mortgage lender, Habitat for Humanity Detroit never made profits more important than people. Habitat doesn't even charge interest on their mortgages.

Nonetheless, the homeless individuals and other low-income folks that Cass serves hadn't been candidates for the local Habitat program. As impressive as Habitat for Humanity was and is, even after satisfying the sweat equity requirements and squirreling away enough money for a down payment plus closing costs, our people earning as little as $9,000 annually couldn't qualify for a mortgage. In short, people who are working part-time jobs or for minimum wages like cooks, waitresses, retail sales people, security guards and custodial staff are stuck renting for decades. The same is true of individuals living on Social Security or Social Security Disability. Many of them (58 percent according to PolicyMap's use of 2011-2015 census data) were paying more than 30 percent of their incomes for housing.[37]

Unable to raise the income for large numbers of poor people, we began exploring how we might instead help them get off the rental treadmill and get on the path for home ownership. It is home ownership—not stocks or bonds or family businesses—which has served as the piggy bank for the nation. I suggested that tiny houses might be the solution. For six months, we developed a business plan for 25 250- to 400-square-foot homes. As part of the process, I used my vacation to visit Quixote Village in Olympia, Washington and Right 2 Dream Too and Caravan-The Tiny House Hotel in Portland, Oregon.

Stacy Conwell-Leigh, who would be named the owner's representative for the project, didn't go to the northwestern states but instead attended a Tumbleweed conference to glean some basic construction information. Aimee Clark, Cass' Finance Director, crunched numbers and our new deputy director, Kim Hudolin, turned her attention to a myriad of legal considerations. By the time the plan was presented to the Cass board of directors in May 2016, we had already secured pre-development funding from the RNR Foundation to purchase architectural plans.

One of the earliest discussions revolved around naming the project. We deliberately retained Cass Community and simply added Tiny Homes. The word "home" hinted that the buildings were more than structures. Conversely, the word "house" implies a building, generally a temporary place such as a birdhouse, a dollhouse, a doghouse, a tree house, a whorehouse, an outhouse, a crack house, a jailhouse or even the White House. These are places to stay for a limited period of time. We clung to the word home because, for us, it signified a residence that is simultaneously a more permanent dwelling and an "emotional" address. It also pointed to the fact that the program was as much about home ownership as it was about tiny living.

The Cass Community name designation points to the fact that the 25 tiny homes have been added to the northern edge of our pedestrian "campus," which is part of an existing neighborhood in the city of Detroit. The location of the homes (and in real estate everything is about location) gives the new residents immediate access to all the services already available through Cass within five or six blocks.

Optional Cass programs and services within walking distance include:

- **AA/NA groups**—Weekly fellowship meetings for people living with addiction.
- **the bike bank**—Residents can borrow bicycles at no cost for an hour, day, weekend, month.
- **a distribution center**—Clothing and furniture.
- **food services and community gardens**—They are eligible for a monthly free box of food and/or a daily hot meal. Residents who don't want to grow vegetables on their own property can access the fresh produce from the community gardens.

- **a computer lab and internet services**—Adults have access to online entertainment, education, job resources, etc.
- **a free medical clinic**—Volunteer physicians and medical students provide primary care including prescriptions and medications for community members. They can also often arrange for pro bono surgeries if required.
- **employment (Green Industries jobs)**—Residents can work at recycling and repurposing wood, paper, cardboard, tires and glass. Employees start at slightly more than the minimum wage and can work for up to 30 hours a week.
- **GED and literacy classes**—Residents can participate in weekly educational classes at the Scott Building.
- **a gymnasium**—Residents can use the weights, stationary bikes, pool and ping pong tables and/or the Wii.
- **a tool warehouse**—Ladders, paint rollers, pans and extension poles, lawn mowers, rakes, shovels, bush trimmers, etc. are available to residents at no charge.
- **the Union**—The canteen carries inexpensive canned goods, beverages, Kleenex, toilet paper, laundry detergent, hygiene products, etc.
- **worship**—In less than a mile, residents are free to worship (or not) with Baptists, Pentecostals, United Methodists or at a mosque. (The Cass mid-week service is held in the World Building or warehouse. Participation is voluntary and typically a choir composed of formerly homeless men, The Ambassadors, lead the music and invited preachers from a variety of denominations deliver the sermon.) Volunteer teams from churches tend to participate with people from the community.

The proximity of the Cass tiny homes to the campus can't be overstated. Twenty-five percent of Detroit households don't have access to a vehicle. The percentage among low-income folks skyrockets because the cost of buying, maintaining, fueling and insuring a vehicle is prohibitive (auto insurance rates in Detroit are twice what they are elsewhere in the region). The city's Department of Transportation (DDOT) buses travel 43 routes but the city is 139,000 square miles and suburban connections are limited. Biking is a viable option (Detroit now has over 100 miles of bike lanes) yet the weather (rain, snow, ice ...) often leaves large numbers of cyclists stranded. The fact that residents are able to walk to food, medical care, recreation, education, employment opportunities and social events is key to providing an urban safety net.

CAMPUS KEY

A. WORLD BUILDING
Administrative Offices,
Medical Clinic,
Store, Publishing House,
Cass Communitea,
and Green Industries

B. SUSAN BATH
THOMASSON BUILDING
& APARTMENTS
Housing for Men
and Women

C. THE SCOTT BUILDING
Family Shelter,
Rotating Shelter,
Permanent Housing,
PATH Offices
and Food Services

D. THE WAREHOUSE
Building Supplies and
Landscaping Equipment
Document Destruction

E. ANTISDEL APARTMENTS
41 Units for Men and Women

F. WESLEY APARTMENTS
4 Family Units

G. VACANT LOTS
New Tiny Homes Development

H. THE GREENHOUSE

I. LITTLETON APARTMENTS
13 Units for Men and Women

J. THE BRADY BUILDING
13 Units for Men and Women

CCSS BUILDINGS
NOT ON CAMPUS
Activity Center and
Cass House

Directions to Cass Community Social Services' World Building

From Pontiac, Rochester and the North:
I-75 South to M-8 West to M-10 South (Lodge) take exit 6B (Elmhurst) to the stop sign. Turn left onto Woodrow Wilson. At the light, turn right onto Webb. At the light at Rosa Parks, jog to the left and continue on Webb to the parking lot on your right.

From Clinton Township, St. Clair Shores, and the East:
I-94 Westbound to M-10 North (Lodge) take exit 6A (Webb). At the light turn left onto Webb. At the second light (Rosa Parks) jog to the left and continue on Webb to the parking lot on your right.

From Ann Arbor, Detroit Metropolitan Airport and the West:
I-94 Eastbound to M-10 North (Lodge) take exit 6A (Webb). At the light turn left onto Webb. At the second light (Rosa Parks) jog to the left and continue on Webb to the parking lot on your right

FIRST TINY HOME
BUILT ON THIS SITE

Tony ████ Doesnt detroit have plenty of empty houses? I think this tiny house crazy is going to peoples heads.
Like · Reply · September 14, 2016 at 12:17am

Bonnie ████ Why don't they utilize the empty schools and buildings and modify them into apartments? Would be way cheaper I think!
Like · Reply · September 14, 2016 at 1:04am

Lori ████ I live in Detroit. I doubt this will happen. And if it does, they won't go to homeless people.
Like · Reply · September 14, 2016 at 3:15pm

Curt ████ Stop all new development. Revitalize the old neighobrhoods instead. We need legislature to prevent developers from buying up farms and turning them into another housing development or strip mall. If we continue with this locust mentality, we will be totally dependent on foreign produce. You don't need a Sims game to figure out that too many houses = less resources and less land for farms.
Like · Reply · September 17, 2016 at 4:59pm

Darron ████ @ Kathy I am so into the tiny house movement. Leaving a small stamp on our environment in an eco friendly manner. Eventually, all people will have to go green to save our planet. Might as well be ahead of the curve.
Like · Reply · September 15, 2016 at 7:20pm

Travis ████ But there is already enough empty house to house them all and still have more .. start placing them.
Like · Reply · September 24, 2016 at 1:39pm

6

Detroit:
Land of Opportunity

CASS PURCHASED A 34,500-square-foot apartment building at the corner of Elmhurst and Woodrow Wilson Streets in 2007 with the hopes of refurbishing the ruined structure and converting it into permanent supportive housing for formerly homeless women and men. Regrettably, the recession, which was particularly severe in Michigan, delayed the renovations for five years because investing in Detroit seemed such a gamble. The project ultimately required several sources of layered funding. Prior to the ribbon-cutting ceremony on November 7, 2013 and, during a year of extensive rehab, the agency discussed with city representatives the possibility of purchasing a number of properties that surrounded the building so that there would be room for a parking lot and future expansion.

The inquiries resulted in Cass acquiring 25 empty lots and one parcel with a dilapidated house. The acquisition cost $15,000. There were only two problems initially with the land acquisition: First, the city didn't close on the parcels until January 21, 2015; and second, the lots were sold without a clear title. Once we owned the properties, a third problem consumed us:

We were unsure if the ground was environmentally safe. What we had learned from other building projects was that environmental testing is a must. Our first residential building, the Scott Building on Woodrow Wilson, had asbestos. Beyond that, we discovered that the first time the basement flooded, the former hospital annex had been flushing used syringes down the toilets. The sewers were clogged with needles and other sharp objects. It took a high-pressure jet system to bore through the metal blockage. The Cass warehouse on the opposite side of Woodrow Wilson sat next to a historic auto shop that was contaminated. The land behind the Arthur Antisdel Apartments had asbestos in the soil that required remediation.

So in May, Cass engaged ASTI Environmental to conduct a Phase I assessment on the tiny homes' parcels. It cost $2,400, but the report, as with the previous ones, helped our leadership better understand the neighborhood and its risks. We learned from the report that residential buildings started appearing in the area after 1915. The first house went up in 1916 and most of the other residences were constructed between 1916 and 1920. The building permits indicate that many of them were two-family structures and many had detached garages.

Properties developed after 1915 in Detroit were connected to municipal water and a sewer system. (The nearest surface water was and is 5.18 miles southwest—the Detroit River.) There was no evidence that the residents ever used septic systems or wells. Water quality can be a real issue. While we were writing the Tiny Homes business plan, the water crisis in Flint was front-page news across the country. We also learned from the Phase I assessment that the Cass Tiny Homes would be 640 feet above sea level.

By reviewing the historical aerial photographs and Sanborn maps, ASTI was able to document the housing history of the area. In the 1950s, the second stretch of the north- and southbound John C. Lodge Freeway took out homes in its path, even some of the Boston-Edison neighborhood mansions south of Cass. Otherwise, houses were on most of the nearby residential lots by the early 1970s. By the mid-'70s, lots began having houses removed. In the early 2000s, when we opened the Scott Building on Woodrow Wilson, only a few houses remained scattered across the four blocks north of our location, and the 2010 photo showed that practically all of those houses were gone. The area had reverted to the fields of 1915.

This history was confirmed by the wreck and remove records that were granted by the city between 1973 and 1977. The building permits were limited to patio covers, fences and a garage in 1974—so once houses were razed, the unoccupied properties remained fallow. Cass Tiny Homes would be the first construction in the area in over 50 years.

The story was repeated for the businesses along Woodrow Wilson. They were also constructed beginning in 1915. A confectioner, a dry goods store, a Salvation Army church, a pool hall, a roofing company, a furniture repair shop, a beauty salon and the National Ladder & Scaffold Co. helped fill out the commercial strip. We had no idea about any of this as not a single business structure stands on the wide street other than a partially boarded-up store-front church.

The report indicated that there were potentially some environmental issues where businesses once stood. By reviewing the oil and tank cards at the Buildings and Safety Department, ASTI learned that two lots had tanks present. One on Richton had a 2,220-gallon heating-oil tank in its basement in 1952 and another on Woodrow Wilson had a 2,275-gallon heating-oil tank outside of the building (likely located above ground) in 1951. These were considered to be a minimal risk.

The Phase I Environmental Site Assessment (ESA) discovered the likely presence of contaminated fill material across the property lots. Therefore, Cass retained ASTI to conduct a Phase II ESA. The cost for this testing was $4,710 and it was conducted in June 2015. This investigation involved extracting 12 soil borings using stainless-steel hand augers to depths of 1 and 2 feet. The samples were tested in a Lansing laboratory for arsenic and lead. One of the properties came back with arsenic but it did not exceed the relevant GRCC (Generic Residential Cleanup Criteria) or the published Michigan Background

Soil Survey data. The remaining lots detected arsenic below the GRCC.

Another sample on Woodrow Wilson came back high for lead. ASTI suggested that we do a few more borings on the property to better delineate the area and have a finite area of excavation to mitigate the problem. We contracted with ASTI in January 2017 to conduct further testing and check for chemical migration that may have occurred from the former dry cleaners and ink manufacturing facility that adjoined the property. The last thing we wanted to do was to create affordable, yet toxic homes. The third assessment took place at a cost of $4,500. It concluded that remediation would be needed. Thus, when we develop that section of the commercial strip, 2 feet of the uppermost soil will have to be removed from a 30-by-30 parcel at a cost of roughly $15,000.

Zoning was never a problem for the project. We requested a meeting with a representative from the Zoning Division prior to any pre-development work. Since we proposed building permanent structures on regular-sized lots (generally 30 by 100 feet) and since Detroit did not have a minimum building size requirement, the organization didn't have to request any variances.

Where we ran into problems had to do with the lot sizes. In August 2016, Cass purchased an additional eight residential properties on Elmhurst, Richton and Monterey from the Detroit Land Bank because some of the original lots were too narrow to accommodate the set back requirements. Today Detroit mandates a minimum of 7 feet on either side of each home. Thus, the width of our homes couldn't exceed 16 feet on most lots and, in some cases, it was necessary to combine more than one lot. The extra land cost another $920 plus a $120 recording fee.

Obtaining a clear title was much more complicated. Kim Hudolin hired a title company to conduct searches for the agency. Even with a recorded deed, we waited until each title was cleared before building on the corresponding property. Having a prior owner contest the title could potentially cost us time and money. Therefore, perfect titles determined the order of construction.

cass community social services
fighting poverty, creating opportunity, building community

2008   2017

Above: The Antisdel Apartment building before and after renovations. Below: The bottom of the picture shows the service drive ramp off of the Lodge Freeway. The light-colored soil in the left corner is where we razed an abandoned building. Next to it, the city of Detroit took down another one at roughly the same time. The parking lot on the left edge of the picture belongs to the Cass Scott Building and the large building at the corner is our Antisdel Apartment building with 41 units of permanent supportive housing for formerly homeless men and women. As you can see, there were no houses left to rehab.

John ▓▓▓▓ Brian I wonder if they're 10x8 with a skylight?
Like · Reply · September 14, 2016 at 12:07am

Niki ▓▓▓▓ This is great! Too bad HUD is already working to make "tiny home living" illegal. They aren't "up to code" they say. F▓▓king vultures.
Like · Reply · September 17, 2016 at 5:39am

Amarja ▓▓▓▓ Good idea, why not make small houses beautifull, small but affordable en like little energyfriendly castle's
Like · Reply · September 14, 2016 at 5:04am

Steve ▓▓▓▓ "Is that up to code?" Helpful government official.
Like · Reply · September 14, 2016 at 10:15am

Tonia ▓▓▓▓ How do you get around the minimum of 1000 square foot ordinance?
Like · Reply · September 14, 2016 at 10:39am

Love ▓▓▓▓ Not going to help out unless you house they're guaranteed to grow without mold
Like · Reply · September 15, 2016 at 11:53am

Cheryl ▓▓▓▓ This is great but not for seniors. The bed is usually on a lofted area with steep steps.
Like · Reply · September 15, 2016 at 6:11pm

Alex ▓▓▓▓ Around my city there are many low income housing option. Houses like these would most likely be tear downs in 30 years for real homeowners. I can't imagine that these would be very energy efficient either with the number of exterior walls to living space.
Like · Reply · September 15, 2016 at 8:03pm

Joe ▓▓▓▓ They should have solar panels too. It would reduce costs for everyone.
Like · Reply · September 21, 2016 at 9:40am

7

Architectural Plans and Environmental Features

OUR FAMILY MOVED from the east side of Detroit to Royal Oak when I was in the sixth grade. For a while, my parents debated between a suburban house in Utica and the one they ultimately selected. Their decision was based on the quality of the Royal Oak schools and the fact the old farmhouse on Eleven Mile had so much character—you might even say charm. The location was not lost on my college friends who joked that I was raised in a truck stop. My mother always wanted to live somewhere that was spacious enough that you could rearrange the furniture. She must have said a million times that she would never have been happy in a cookie-cutter house where everyone driving down the street knew where your sofa sat.

Our 100-year-old, two-story wood house was roomy because previous owners had enlarged it over time with multiple additions. I am convinced that none of them consulted an architect. The front porch reminded you of the end of *Beetlejuice*. There wasn't a single right angle anywhere. If you dropped a marble on the floor, there was no telling where it would end up. We used to store pop and Jell-O on the window-rich porch because it was always about 20 degrees colder than the rest of the house. Years later we discovered that the heat piping ran from the furnace to the closed-in porch through about 10 feet that was on the outside of the house. Without insulation for 50-some years, the warm air turned cold before it reached the porch's floor vent. There wasn't any insulation in the walls either. This was not a problem, since winter was only *one* of our seasons. All the water pipes were installed along the north wall (meaning they weren't heated by sunlight) and during extremely cold winters, we used hair dryers to keep them from freezing over.

If you are romanticizing about an episode of *This Old House* I would warn you that each of our home-improvement projects— because there were no architectural plans—involved discoveries and delays. While we refinished three rooms with hardwood floors, we found that each job included a surprise under the carpeting: trap doors, painted-on rugs and patches filled with concrete.

The house next door, which belonged to the Erwins, was smaller and newer. They had seven children and, I suspect, an architect. Their ground was built up, elevated about two feet above our lot. The two driveways were parallel to each other so that every time it rained, all their runoff pooled up in the Fowler driveway. Our flooded cement could have been used as an "after" photograph for a monsoon insurance claim.

With this history, I was surprised by the reaction of many friends and volunteers when we insisted that every Cass Tiny Home would be different inside and out. One suburban architect invited us to his home to see the work he was doing in affluent communities with pocket neighborhoods. It would save Cass a fortune, he argued, to pick three or four models and simply repeat them to make up the 25 homes. I thought to myself how predictable and boring that would be. It would be institutional, I thought, unappealing to the eye. I felt that having a unique house would instill pride in people who have had to settle for uniform everything. I could hear my mother remarking about the floor plan and the sofa.

"I want every house to be different, distinctive and attractive. They should be interesting and inviting. The smaller sizes shouldn't change that. We will have to find other ways to save money," I said and he walked away from the project.

Stacy Conwell-Leigh was equally frustrated with my decision but, since she drew a paycheck from Cass, she generally kept it to herself. One way to stretch our dollars was to purchase plans rather than hire an architect to create new designs. Stacy, our summer college interns and I all began surfing the Internet to find examples of tiny houses that were both visually appealing and energy-efficient. I liked the idea of using home plans that had already been built somewhere else, too, because products are perfected over time as customers report any kinks and personal preferences.

What we found is that people have very different ideas about what constitutes a tiny house. Some were as large as 1,200 square feet and others just 50. We also discovered that most of the houses online were mobile, to be constructed on trailers, like those on HGTV. The group narrowed its scope to stationary houses between 250 and 400 square feet and identified our first home almost immediately. It was a stunning Tudor design embellished with a stone fireplace and chimney.

Repetitive searching located other striking home styles: a Cape Cod, a Victorian and a Katrina Cottage. We purchased the plans for a craftsman, a contemporary home, a recycled house that utilized old barn wood and even a tower studio that we called "the lighthouse." Finding 25 different plans was harder than we initially imagined. It required nearly a year. The cost of the drawings ranged from $300 to $1,500, a fraction of the price tag for engaging an architectural firm. Many of the plans were obtained digitally through Houseplans.com. Daniel Gregory, the editor-in-chief at Houseplans in San Francisco, was extremely helpful in the process.

A few of the houses we liked from the Internet were "fake residences." They were actually office buildings, playhouses and potting sheds. They were like the old movie sets with nothing behind them. They didn't have blueprints. There were no floor plans to establish the placement of windows, walls and doors. Who could guess the ceiling heights or the floor materials? We were missing the measurements for the kitchens and bathrooms. Three different times we gave a photo to an architect and asked him/her if they could produce drawings for us because we liked the picture (façade) so much. We met Ed Weir at a peace conference sponsored by the Rotary Club in Ann Arbor and he took our snapshot and designed a beautiful Victorian home.

A few of the plans were created for us for free without photos, too. Naseem Alizadeh from the Bureau for Architecture and Urbanism stopped in during her Thanksgiving trip to visit family and offered to design a house for the project—and ended up designing three different homes. Bob Berard organized a design challenge at Quinn Evan Architects. His colleagues submitted original tiny house drawings from Washington D.C. and Chicago as well as Detroit. We ended up using a number of their blueprints. What's more, several generous architects gifted us their work so we are now able to sell the plans to others who want to build one of the homes.

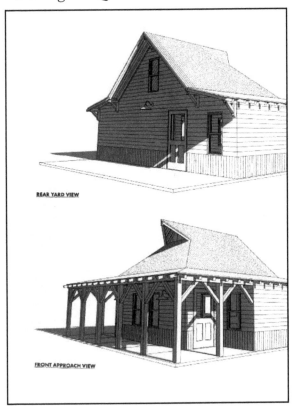

Also, two architects from

This is one of the concept drawings from Quinn Evans Architects.

the Windy City's Antunovich Associates Terry Howell and Lon Stousland and a partner from the firm Via Chicago Marty Sandberg had recently won the AIA Chicago Tiny Homes Competition for a design called, "A House for Living In." We procured their house plans at a bargain-basement price, modified the interior slightly and added it to our collection.

You have to be careful about using architectural plans from different climates, states and countries. For instance, one set of drawings originated in Florida. Obviously the roofing in the Sunshine State doesn't need to account for snow loads. In Michigan, it is a must. Moreover, we learned that modifying floor plans to make the best use of building materials was also worth the expense. For instance, by adding or subtracting a couple of inches, we could use full sheets of drywall and lessen much of the cutting, taping and mudding, etc. By eliminating smaller slivers, we reduced material waste by 90 percent.

Customizing the interiors was made infinitely easier because we had interns helping us from area colleges. Katie Mercier, a design student at Baker College, was more than happy to make the homes livable. She moved walls and added windows. Her adaptations included barn doors and pocket doors, ceiling fans and fold-out furniture. She asked intelligent questions about building materials as well as researched corporate foundations that might be interested in funding the project. Even though she was working and attending school, Katie drove to Cass from Bay City (100 miles each way) twice a week.

Corissa Green lived closer. She hailed from Wayne State University's Department of Urban Studies & Planning. At Cass, she interfaced with designers and connected with local artists to acquire art for the Tiny Homes. In addition to digging deep into the tiny house plans, Corissa organized a fundraiser at the restaurant she managed, Lily's Seafood Grill and Brewery, in Royal Oak. It was common to see her chasing down retailers to persuade them to donate gift cards and other items to be auctioned off in support of our development.

Our very first intern was Krystal Hull from the University of Michigan-Dearborn. Krystal went above and beyond keeping the mountains of donated building materials organized in the warehouse, supervising skilled and unskilled volunteer groups and helping to install the very first deck. Her internship ended in August, but she continued to participate in events for nine more months. Eventually she hopes to build a tiny house for herself and a separate one for her boyfriend.

We made a few design decisions early on. Only a couple of the homes would include lofts for sleeping areas. As people age, stairs can become problematic. (We tried to minimize entryway stairs for the homeowners as well as for their visitors.) Several of the homes took advantage of upper areas for storage. It was also determined that we'd build every house with a usable front porch or a back deck or patio in order to increase the living space. In Michigan we have four seasons: fall, winter, spring and construction. Three of our seasons are good for barbeques and card games, reading and catching up with neighbors.

We were clear from the onset that energy efficiencies should be included in the architectural designs. Thus there are plenty of double-pane windows with high R-values that passively provide light and warmth from the sun. The selection of building materials also played into our pro-environment philosophy. We used spray foam insulation, which sealed off the nooks and crannies that typically allow air to escape. (As much as 40 percent of a building's energy is lost due to air infiltration.) All of the appliances are ENERGY STAR certified. The toilets and fixtures are low-flow or water-conserving. The hot water is on-demand. Residents have the option of rainwater harvesting.

The Cass homes are not Net Zero, meaning that they do not produce as much energy as they use. Geothermal was cost prohibitive. Our research into using wind turbines to provide outside lighting recognized that there were basic challenges. Each turbine needed to be 30 feet above all the other obstructions and at least 90 feet in the air. According to city code, the towers would have to have land enough so that they wouldn't hit something if they fell (at least 200 by 200 feet). Even if we had appropriate space, the average wind in Detroit is barely sufficient to justify the costs. A local wind energy feasibility study noted that in order to increase performance, a turbine in Detroit would need to be 264 feet in the air. Originally we nixed PV (solar) panels because we were concerned about theft. Halfway through the construction phase, we changed our minds and mounted solar arrays at each home. There is solar lighting in the alleys, as well.

Beyond this, several environmental factors should be mentioned. The small building footprints allowed us to work around the existing trees. Whenever possible, we repurposed donated building materials. Moreover, the agency operates a recycling center that accepts paper, cardboard and cans. The tiny homes residents simply drop these items off at the building on Woodrow Wilson. Will Cass win the Al Gore environmental innovation award? No. But Cass Tiny Homes are a vast improvement over the energy guzzling houses that comprise most of our domestic housing stock.

Above: The Nickelsville Ballard solar panels were purchased by the local Rotary. They produce four hours of energy a day. Since Cass Tiny Homes rely on electricity exclusively, we installed grid-direct solar systems and designed small, stand alone solar battery–based generators so that residents would have access to power during emergencies.

WHAT A DIFFERENCE RESIDENTIAL SIZE MAKES

AVERAGE HOUSE   VS   TINY HOUSE

AVERAGE HOUSE SIZE IN 2015

2657 SF [1]

It takes about 7 1/2 logging hours to provide lumber for an average house [3]

The average house has 46 light bulbs consuming 653 Wh of electricity [9]

653 KWH

---

25 - 40 % of solid waste stream is construction related [4]

In the U.S. buildings account for 72% of total electricity used [5]

Buildings create 38% of the nation's total carbon dioxide [6]

The average home size has increased by 61% in the last 40 years [7]

Laid end-to-end, lumber to build a 3k SF house would stretch 4 miles [8]

Construction of hoouses accounts for 3/4 of lumber used yearly in U.S. [10]

15% of greenhouse gases come from residential houses [11]

AVERAGE CASS TINY HOME

325 SF [2]

It takes about 7/8 logging hours to provide lumber for a Cass Tiny Home

The average Cass Tiny Home has 7 light bulbs consuming 99.4 Wh of electricity

99.4 KWH

Consumption of fossil fuels has contributed significantly to the degradation of our environment. Global warming, climate change, extinction of wildlife species, depletion of the ozone layer, and increased levels of pollution are some of the problems we face. The release of CO_2 into our atmosphere is the largest contributor to global warming.

This work is licensed under a Creative Commons Attribution-NonCommercial-NoDerivitives 4.0 International License

Design of infographic by Gabriella from tinyHouseBuild

CO2 AND OUR ENVIRONMENT

AVERAGE HOUSE IN 2015	VS	AVERAGE CASS TINY HOME

⚡ ELECTRICITY ⚡

13,067 kWH/yr [13]

Since the industrial Revolution, CO2 in the atmosphere is higher than at any time in the past 100 million years [14]

1,598 kWH/yr [*]

🔥 HEATING 🔥

363 pounds CO2 [15]

More than 1 M species have become extinct due to th eeffects of global warming [16]

2,002 pounds CO2 [*]

❄ COOLING ❄

82 pounds CO2 [17]

Since 1870. global sea levels have risen by roughly 8" [18]

1,001 pounds CO2 [*]

Cass Tiny houses can save 26,000 pounds of CO2 per year from going into the atmosphere

TOTAL: 28,636 POUNDS

By living in a Cass Tiny house, you can significantly decrease the burden you place on resources

TOTAL: 3,503 POUNDS

WINNER!

: 1 http://articles.chicagotribune.com/2014-06-02/business/chi-average-home-size-sets-new-record-20140603_1_home-size-home-builders-new-record 2 http://thetinylife.com/tiny-house-
·/ 3 http://www.idahoforests.org/woodhous.htm 4 http://www.aia.org/aiaucmp/groups/secure/documents/pdf/aiap072739.pdf 5,6 http://www.epa.gov/greenbuilding/pubs/gbstats.pdf 7 http://www.
rg/2014/02/todays-new-homes-are-1000-square-feet-larger-than-in-1973-and-the-living-space-per-person-has-doubled-over-last-40-years/ 8 http://www.alternet.org/story/61523/big_houses_are_
%3A-america's_mcmansion-problem 9,10 http://www.cbsnews.com/news/green-light-bulb-buying-guide/ 11 http://www.livescience.com/4092-real-green-house-heating-bill-25-years 12 http://
com/earth-matters/climate-weather/stories/co2-101-why-is-carbon-dioxide-bad#ixzz3GbxlqZSt 13 http://www.energyville.com/sourcesanddemands/residentialhomes/ 14 http://forces.si.edu/
e/02_04_07.html 15 http://www.cartalk.com/content/global-warming-and-your-car-0 16 http://www.conserve-energy-future.com/various-global-warming-facts.php#sthash.meUpX5g.dpuf 17 http://
gov/greenhomes/WholeHouse.htm 18 https://www.dosomething.org/facts/11-facts-about-global-warminghttps://www.dosomething.org/facts/11-facts-about-global-warminghttps://www.dosomething.
1-facts-about-global-warming

Stephen ▓▓▓▓ I think the home should be much smaller and they really do not need a backyard I like that idea someone said of the homeless help building them as a small down payment a lot of homeless will struggle with paying a small and not a ring no matter how much it is I really feel like a skyscraper would be better to be built and with tiny apartments that each homeless person could stay in
Like · Reply · January 23, 2017 at 11:17pm

Jeffrey ▓▓▓▓ The near-perfect solution for depressed neighborhoods.
Like · Reply · September 18, 2016 at 9:45am

Eva ▓▓▓▓ this is wonderful. its about time.
Like · Reply · September 14, 2016 at 3:13pm

8

Foundations

THE INSIDE OF the house on Eleven Mile had nooks and crannies and cupboards everywhere. I was always envious of my older brothers' bedroom because it had cherry paneling and the beds were built into opposite walls of the room with nightlights tucked in for reading. But the place I avoided was the basement. Since the house went up in stages, the basement floor had more than one level and it was always very dark and damp downstairs. On the north end of it, there was a root cellar from back in the days before there was decent refrigeration or food distribution. Evidently, the early homeowners stored their root vegetables in the unlit room so they would have ample food throughout the nonproductive winter months. As far as I know, we never used it. My mother worked at Meijer, a Michigan grocery store.

The root cellar protruded off the back of the house into the backyard. With a curved cement top, the cellar stood about 4 feet tall and roughly 10 feet away from the above-ground pool. I perched my nephew up on top when he was a toddler. "OK," I said standing relatively close (although I'm sure he sized up the distance in light years). "Jump. Come on, I'll catch you." Again, I prompted him, "Jump!"

You could see the gears of his young mind turning like the mechanisms of a wristwatch displayed through a clear back. He wanted to leap, but fear kept him fixed on top of the empty tomb-like food closet. "Jump," I encouraged him as I extended my arms. It took constant coaxing, but finally he took flight. His eyes were closed because for him it was like vaulting off the observation deck of the Empire State Building. He trusted me.

What we called the fruit cellar, also in the unfinished basement, wasn't to be confused with a root cellar or a wine cellar. The root cellar was intended to keep food from freezing in the winter and to prevent it from spoiling in the summer. The fruit cellar was crammed full of shelves that held jars of jelly and preserves: strawberry, grape and apple. It held pickles and tomatoes—all in clear glass containers, most with paraffin wax on top and a few with lids attached by rings. It was also served as a pantry for store-bought canned goods and paper products—and my nephew.

My brother's family stayed with my parents in the house in Royal Oak for a while. He was going through a divorce and so my folks occupied the first floor and my brother and his children took over the second floor. The problem was that at that point in their relationship, my brother and my teenage nephew weren't getting along. After about two weeks of verbal confrontations, my mother suggested that my nephew move down to the fruit cellar. It was 5 by 10 feet with a 6-foot ceiling, just enough room for a twin bed and an alarm clock if he put it by the tuna fish. That small, doorless space gave him some privacy, peace and quiet, and helped him realize that he could live in harmony with his father as long as they had a floor between them.

We never entertained the idea of sinking basements below the Tiny Homes. Basements in Michigan for detached houses have traditionally been used to store the boiler, hot water heater, a fuse box and laundry machines. Since we didn't need a large amount of square footage to accommodate these items, it wouldn't have been a good return on our investment.

So, after only a few minor alterations, we submitted our first one-story drawing for approval. The building department then asked for mechanical, electrical and plumbing drawings for the construction permit. They don't always require these but, of course, in our case they did. We paid a local firm to create the technical drawings and presented paperwork a second time. Next, the city representative said it was necessary for a master plumber to pull the utility permits. We paid for him to take the documents down to the City-County Building, a 20-story facility now named for the former Mayor Coleman A. Young, but when he arrived the Municipal Center was locked down for the day because a visitor had been detected carrying a weapon (fortunately, no one was injured.)

Once the permit was finally issued, the construction crew began digging a hole into which they could pour a deep foundation for the first tiny home. Their excavating equipment was no match for what was beneath the ground however. Just below the surface, the backhoes and front-end loaders churned up huge rocks, cinder blocks and giant slabs of concrete. What no one knew prior to starting the pit was that when houses were demolished in the 1970s and 1980s, the city allowed the bulk of the debris to be buried in the basements and covered with a thin layer of soil.

I considered starting a rumor that Queen Nefertiti was interred in one of the 25 lots but decided instead to use a slab-on-grade foundation. This procedure first outlined the house using a backhoe to dig 42 inches down around the perimeter. Next, plywood was used to form the foundation walls due to the instability of the existing soil and concrete was poured to make the footings. Once this was completed, cinder blocks were added and the underground water and sanitary lines were run after core holes were drilled to bring them into the house. Finally, the concrete was poured in a mold and cured. The good news was that this type of foundation is sturdy and termite-proof.

One objection to using a slab-on-grade foundation was the cost of concrete. It ran $12,000-$15,000 a house for the foundation. The general contractor recommended switching to a conventional crawlspace foundation to reduce the expenses and to provide easy future access to the electrical or plumbing lines. We decided to stay with the slab-on-grade because we felt it would provide a better barrier to pests/rodents, it would require less elevation from the ground (needing only one or two steps) and because the slab could help insulate the house. When the plumber read the plan for the Sugar Magnolia house upside down and put all of the utilities in backwards, we discovered that a jackhammer was required to fix the mix-up.

What we learned from the first batch of six houses is that cold weather provides a challenge to utilizing concrete slabs. When it was time to start construction, the work crew took off two weeks for the start of hunting season (who knew?) and when they returned we were told that they would need three consecutive days of temperatures above 40 degrees Fahrenheit to pour the foundations. Enter Richard Scheck, from Frank Rewold and Son, Inc. in Rochester, Michigan. Rich is a LEED accredited (Leadership in Environmental and Energy Design) engineer who has managed $700,000,000 worth of building projects. He volunteered to help with Cass Tiny Homes by reviewing plans, billings and soliciting donations from area contractors. He schooled us about how to use chemical accelerators, heaters and blankets so that the foundations weren't delayed for months.

Above: The cinder-block wall outlines the first Cass home.
Right: With the slab-on-grade poured and smoothed
out, the building was attached to the foundation.

John ████ Its Detroit it will get burned down or be robbed all the time. Its the truth, this would just be a waste of time. Take the homeless send to another country, have them come back to the United States and they will have insurance, bridge card and a roof over there head some where else. Dam shame we cant help our own people.

Its like cooking dinner for your family but you feed the neighbors instead.
Like · Reply · September 14, 2016 at 11:04pm

Helen ████ Good luck ••' watch your back !And mostly lock your car 🦎🦎🦎 grew up there left came back lived there 20 more yrs
Car stolen out of drive way!!!moved Up North 😊
Like · Reply · September 17, 2016 at 9:18am

Guersom ████ Uh no there's violence over there before going in that zone there's a wall that says entered on your own risk
Like · Reply · September 17, 2016 at 11:20pm

Isaac ████ Just make sure to build a dam wall around them so drug addicts can't get in and steal the wiring and end up having them catch fire and burn like the thousands of houses do every year in detroit.
Like · Reply · September 20, 2016 at 6:45pm

9

Guarding the Copper

IN THE 1970S most freshmen at Albion College lived in
Wesley Hall on the north side of campus. The building was
named for John and Charles Wesley's mother, Susanna. (Actually, she was the mother of 19 children, not just the founder of
Methodism and his hymn-writing brother. Nine of Susanna's
children died as infants including two sets of twins.) The Wesley dorm is a three-story, brick colonial-style building with an
expansive circular drive that begins and ends on Michigan Avenue. East and west additions were added to the 1925 building in
1956 creating a horseshoe shape. Occasionally men from one of
the fraternities would use the back lawn venue between the east
and west wings to serenade the female residents at night.

When I entered Albion, it was the first time in my life I had
to share a bedroom (one of the benefits of being an only girl). It
took some adjusting to "double-occupancy" on my part. When
could the lights be on or off? What volume of music was acceptable and when? Which musical artists were preferred? I was
nocturnal and my freshman roommate took 8 a.m. calculus
classes. More than that, Barb was one of the rare undergraduates

who actually got up in time to shower, blow her hair dry and use the curling iron before she went to the cafeteria for breakfast. (I was content sleeping in and feeding myself anything leftover in our 1.6-cubic-foot refrigerator.)

Nevertheless, my anxiety about living with someone else was nothing compared to my trepidation related to using a community lavatory. There was only one bathroom for the entire east wing of rooms. Around 30 women used the large restroom which had a wall of toilets in stalls, an internal row of pedestal sinks that stood under gigantic mirrors and a third wall of shower cubicles. Two common pranks took place in the community bathroom. One was that women would remove the clothes from the changing area outside the shower so that when the person who was showering stepped out, her garments would be gone. Her options at that point were to solicit help from anyone else in the bathroom or to race back to her room in a towel. Occasionally, cruel "clothes bandits" also commandeered the towel.

The other shower stunt was less dramatic but potentially more dangerous. Once a bather turned on the shower, another person or posse would quickly run down the row of toilets, flushing every one (this was prior to our commitment to water conservation). The act would temporarily demand all of the cold water available and the unsuspecting person shampooing her hair would be momentarily sprayed with scalding hot water. You really couldn't avoid the hot water shock treatment by taking a warm bath because there was only one tub for all those residents.

Most people didn't want to sit in bathwater anyway. The college, so resourceful in almost every way, had well water with a high concentration of iron at that time. It had a distasteful smell. It wasn't much good for laundry either. Albion is where I started using scented fabric softener. But the place where well water was most noticeable was students' hair. As the academic year progressed, blonde students started to show an orange rust tint to their locks that grew darker each month like a mood ring.

I loved attending Albion. A small, private college, approximately 90 miles west of Detroit, the professors were kind, intelligent and accessible. They would regularly invite classes over to their homes for dinner and take students out for coffee or pizza at a restaurant to discuss course assignments. The natural beauty of campus was spectacular, especially when the oak and elm leaves changed colors in the fall. Generally, it was quiet—except when the church bells tolled on the hour, a train blew its whistle as it rambled across the edge of campus or the marching band announced the start of a football game in the stadium next to the Kalamazoo River.

In time, I learned to live in accord with a roommate. We made friends in the hall. Many nights were spent down in the lounge eating popcorn and typing papers. Barb and I decorated our corner room with matching bedspreads and a life-sized poster of Robert Redford. We each became involved in separate activities, too. She joined the Professional Management (Pro Man) Business Institute and I was drawn to the student publications. Another Wesley freshman and I would spend hours several evenings a week cranking out narrative and printing black and white pictures. It never dawned on us that returning to Wesley after midnight could be dangerous.

Then, one fall afternoon, we learned that a woman from our floor had been attacked. The news was alarming. We all sat cross-legged, lotus-style on the floor in the lounge talking with her about the incident and, then committed to escorting her around campus until the local police could catch the assailant. Pairing up, we walked her to class, to meals and to interviews with campus safety. We practiced holding our keys between our fingers, with key heads in our balled up fists and jagged edges exposed, to stab the man in his eyes. We consulted self-defense books and "trained" so we could deliver a powerful punch or kick to the aggressor.

Nevertheless, he cornered her unattended in the laundry room in the basement. There were two more occurrences after that when she returned to the floor, disheveled and bloodied. We couldn't believe how skilled the goon was at catching her at the rare times that she didn't have a shadow. We devised our own "LoJack" tracking system so someone would always know where the woman was. Security became our obsession. Then, after three nervous weeks, the resident assistant told us that our dorm mate had never been raped or attacked at all. She had contrived the whole story—even cutting and bruising herself—for attention.

The college administration and counseling staff intervened. She went home to her state of origin for the professional help that she needed. The women on our floor spent weeks debriefing the episode but by Christmas we were as focused on finals as everyone else. I signed up to be a resident assistant at Albion (RAs get single rooms) for both my junior and senior years, helping freshmen make the transition to college life—academically, socially, emotionally and physically. What is true is that the college and the city of Albion were generally safe and uneventful.

The same thing couldn't be said for Cass Tiny Homes. The need for security came sooner than we anticipated. Once the utilities were run into the foundation of the first house, we were surprised to see that the copper pipe for water came up through the middle of the concrete floor. Resembling a snake charmed tall by the sound of a piper's music, the copper stood about 3 feet in the air, erect for everyone to see and someone to steal. People periodically die for copper piping in Detroit. A few years ago, one man was electrocuted in the process of snatching copper off of an electrical pole just blocks south of the Cass campus. The thieves who stole millions of dollars worth of copper off brand new streetlights along I-94 in 2013 weren't hurt, but they left drivers in the dark for an extended stretch on the east side expressway. Right after catalytic converters, copper is king for scrappers.

Once we saw the copper pipe, our summer interns were enlisted to monitor the site until the house shell could be built to conceal it. The college students taped a cardboard box over the pipe because it was easier to watch in the dark. When the pipes were set up in the next six homes, though, the interns were back at their respective schools and we were forced to hire temporary security staff to provide surveillance. Like watching the grass grow, it was a monotonous job. Once the houses concealed the piping, we let the crew go. Then, on Easter night, crooks kicked in the doors of all seven homes. They bent the exposed copper pipes until they broke off. Beyond that, the burglars absconded with the PTAC (heating and cooling) units from all seven homes and a refrigerator, a washer/dryer and even the rugs and towels from the "model" home. Without electricity yet, the house alarms were useless.

We had to re-hire security personnel to watch the homes round-the-clock for months. The crime stopped. Detectives from Detroit's Tenth Precinct were able to arrest the thieves by examining our security video footage from one of our other buildings and, miraculously, they recovered the stolen appliances. During the early morning hours of a midnight shift, one of the staff members took some new video footage that captured uninvited visitors to the tiny homes. Two deer showed up without fanfare. Another night a fox was spotted running between the homes. Prior to this, the closest thing to wildlife we'd ever observed in our urban neighborhood had been pheasants.

The pressing question for our development team was: What do we do once the homes are occupied to keep the residents and their property safe? In many Detroit areas, houses are protected by steel bars on the windows and grates on the doors. A few metropolitan neighborhoods are gated communities. We opted to install alarm systems that backed up the dead bolts with sensors that detect an open door or a broken window. Thus the people and their possessions would be secure without causing anyone to feel like they were part of a super-max prison. Each system is monitored and connected to Pointe Alarm, whose staff alerts the Detroit police about any suspicious activities. In addition, there are panic buttons and each detached house is hardwired to detect smoke and/or fire. (All too often, residents who resort to burglar bars and grated doors get trapped inside burning buildings until firefighters can forcibly remove the security devices.)

Stacy Conwell-Leigh researched our alarm options. In addition to keeping the outlay for installation reasonable, we had to be frugal in terms of the monitoring costs. The good news is that New Orleans isn't the only city with saints. Tim Weldon is one of them. He owns the company we chose. The fee for the monthly monitoring was just $25 (around half the average cost in the area). Stacy asked him why he was willing to offer such a discounted rate. Here was his answer:

Good evening Stacy.

I have been a recovering drug addict for over 20 years. I have had many successes since the day I decided to admit I was powerless. There were many hard challenges along the way. The journey could have never taken me this far if it were not for the help of many people along the way. It cannot be done alone. They say "a problem shared is a problem cut in half" I am grateful to be part of the Little Homes Project. The only way to keep sobriety and sanity is to give back. I have found it is the only way to ensure ongoing success for me. If I can be even a small part of assisting another human being to a better life, then I will be that much further in my own personal success and sobriety. You can count on me to be there for the project as long as you will have me. I promise a hard day of work and a helping hand.

Thank you,

Tim

Above: Susanna Wesley Hall at Albion College. The pillared porch faces Michigan Avenue and the twin wings extend back away from the road. Below: One of the Detroit Police officers dusted for fingerprints after the robbery. The detectives from the Detroit Police Department Tenth Precinct deserve credit for solving the crime and returning our stolen goods. After the break-in, many police officers wrote up their reports parked in their squad cars on the streets in front of our Tiny Homes.

John ████ Should of just did a cargo box apartment duplex or something geez building up vertical and horizontal. Would hold more of a larger capacity then a few homes , less money and space ,
Like · Reply · September 14, 2016 at 3:13pm

Renee's ████ If the homeless are not building the homes themselves, they should be.
Like · Reply · September 16, 2016 at 6:46pm

TheNew ████ I've watched them build one off of Elmhurst and the Lodge and its beautiful!!!!
Like · Reply · October 16, 2016 at 12:44pm

10

Framing and Building

BETWEEN 1908 AND 1940, people bought and built 100,000 kit houses in the United States. The kits included architectural plans and 10,000 to 30,000 pieces that were pre-cut, numbered, packaged and shipped to the customers for them to assemble. Folks would pick out the style they wanted from the Sears catalogue and order a nearly complete house. (Montgomery Ward and several other stores sold them, too, including two in Bay City, Michigan).

It reminds me of the model cars and airplanes my brothers would assemble. The miniature parts were likewise numbered and the kits contained directions in extremely small print. Sometimes when my siblings were done putting the models together, there were pieces left over. The thing that really sticks out in my mind, though, was the rancid odor of the glue that emanated from the basement where they toiled over the models. Our executive staff had a world of trouble just following the directions to construct four petite pieces of furniture purchased from IKEA for the Tiny Homes. Build a house?! Really.

We decided to use professional trades to lay the foundation and assemble the frames of our homes. A general contractor had the responsibility of hiring the workers and overseeing their assignments. Although the city didn't demand signed architectural plans, licensed plumbers and electricians were required to pull permits and pass the multiple inspections.

It was incredible to watch the first house being built. We had a webcam on the lot and watched from our respective offices as beams for the walls were lifted up around the slab of concrete like raising a barn. Plywood was applied; then the sectioned roof was hoisted above the frame. A house-wrap material was attached to the exterior walls and, finally, beige eifs that resembled stucco was applied. The windows and door took longer to arrive and install. Moving inside, 6-inch-thick insulation was stuffed between the studs. A small team hung 16-foot sheets of drywall that were taped, mudded and sanded smooth. Vinyl plank flooring went down as quickly as the walls went up. Cultured stone was installed outside as if the home had a fireplace. Finally, cabinets, appliances and the assembled pieces of furniture were put in place after the painting was done.

Each Cass Tiny Home is equipped with a stove, refrigerator, microwave and a combination washer/dryer machine commonly found in Europe. PTAC (Packaged Terminal Air Conditioner) units supply both heat and air-conditioning. They resemble the ones used by hotels with the controls inside and an outdoor louver that is flush with the exterior of the house. Ceiling fans were installed to push the warm air back down into the living space. The first seven houses used smaller stoves but the rest of the homes incorporated standard-size models because they didn't demand as much carpentry work. The microwaves were mounted above the stoves to maximize precious counter space. After the first house, we selected larger apartment-sized refrigerators because people pointed out that they wanted more space in order to limit grocery store trips.

Our other early lessons learned included:

- Alter the floor plans when necessary to use standard-sized windows and doors both for the economy and the ease of replacement.

- Use pavers rather than concrete for the front walkway. It was cheaper, better for drainage and creates an attractive approach.

- Pay the extra amount for spray foam insulation. It costs about three times as much as the fiberglass rolls but it does a superior job of controlling the temperature *and* acting as a sound barrier. The Cass Tiny Homes are next to a major expressway and, yet, when the doors and windows are closed, the sound is muffled, unnoticeable.

- Use two-by-sixes rather than two-by-fours despite the extra expense and loss of square footage because you need enough room for insulation and pipes.

- Take photos of the open walls to capture the position of electrical wiring and plumbing pipes before the insulation and dry wall is installed.

- Remember that conditions elsewhere may impact building supplies. For instance, during our builds hurricanes significantly increased the cost of both lumber and shingles.

The initial projections were that homes could be completed in five weeks. It took nearly four months on the first one, and construction of the next six took an eternity. As mentioned, hunting season shut us down as did extremely cold winter temperatures. But the biggest obstacle involved the utility lines. It took eight months to be hooked up for electricity. Spraying insulation and finishing drywall required a heated house. Just when we were resigned to pay for industrial generators, the cold spell broke and we completed the six shells without power.

One final note, most of the houses have cathedral ceilings. This makes the homes seem paradoxically spacious. The vertical room also affords plenty of prospects for extra shelving, large artwork or a flat screen TV on the walls. The sloping sides of the ceilings further allow for attractive hanging lights.

The original development team (left to right in the photo above: Sam Knolton (general contractor), Jeffery Lockledge (logistics) and Richard Scheck (LEED Engineer).

Above, left to right: The Marie Colvin, the Modern and the Katrina Cottage were built on Richton Street. Below: The side view of the Detroit Junior League Loring Bungalow on Monterey illustrates the height of the cathedral ceiling. It is a dramatic design element for a tiny home.

Wayne ▮▮▮▮ Urban institute, developers, hunders of cities who have tried the same exact thing in different forms, and common sense alike will all tell you that the numbers simply do not add up trying to give everyone their own unit and make it affordable. Neither does it address homelessness at a fundamental/causal level, rather it just strives to shove people back into a smaller and lesser version of the same way of life which got them there in the first place by any unsustainable means neccessary.

Pack a warehouse full of beds and charge RENT!! People are homeless not helpless and they need options not help. You can fit 2-4 broke people in the same space as one by recognizing that privacy is non-essential when push comes to shove.

2-3 people in a room is an awkward silence and feeling of intrusion, but 200-300 in a room is less personal. It also has the benefit of not being claustrophobic.

Missions/charity are flawed in the sense they allow anyone in without screening. The end result is everyone suffers because of a few bad apples. Full grown adults have 6 pm curfews and are told to lie down, shut up, and lay still until it is time to get kicked out at 6 am. But being without property is not a crime, and if cities are going to obstruct individuals natural right to make for themselves outside, then they must provide alternatives which do not reduce people to prison like treatment.

Cities should be MAKING money off of the problem.
Departitionedhousing.com
Like · Reply · September 17, 2016 at 1:02am

Zach ▮▮▮▮ I think this is ridiculous. No one should help anyone, any time, under any circumstances...Especially homeless people
Like · Reply · September 21, 2016 at 6:28pm

Jason ▮▮▮▮ Great idea! Only thing I don't like is that volunteers are required to "worship" as stated on the application. Don't know what that's all about. Must be for some crooked funding requirement. Great for religious volunteers though.
Like · Reply · September 23, 2016 at 7:32pm

11

Donated Labor

WHEN IT WAS time for me to attend seminary, I learned that Boston University (BU) had a very limited number of dorm rooms for School of Theology students. So, for the first time in my life, I rented an apartment. Actually, I shared an apartment because rental property was exorbitantly expensive in Bean Town. During my three years out East, I stayed in four different apartments, house-sat in a couple of amenity-loaded suburban homes and helped to open a post-release house for men coming out of prison.

Each of the apartments—in Boston, Brookline and Newton—were accessible by the Massachusetts Bay Transportation Authority, known as the "T." The Green Line snaked through traffic along Commonwealth Avenue from BU to my first place. The two-bedroom apartment was at the summit of a small hill. We were on the third floor and there was no elevator. Carrying furniture and, later, groceries up was a cardio workout.

Beyond the "mountain climbing," the thing I remember most about the building was that it was infested with pests. If you went into the bathroom at night and turned on the light, it would send several dozen cockroaches scurrying in every direction. The landlord did pay for pest control. Before each exterminator visit everything had to be shifted away from the walls. Even the dishes had to be removed from the cupboards and cabinets so the poison spray could be applied. My roommate would have to remove her dog for the day, which seemed a shame especially since the process never really eliminated the insects. The scrappy, bomb-resistant bugs simply migrated between units.

My second apartment was free of insects but crowded with fellow seminarians. People slept on sofas and futons. It was an effortless way to save money. Besides, everyone was working and/ or attending summer classes. Probably the only time we were all together was to watch an episode of *M*A*S*H* or *Hill Street Blues*. Located in Brookline, the unit wasn't far from BU. It was also relatively close to President Kennedy's birthplace. No, he wasn't born in one of Boston's hospitals. JFK entered the world in a bedroom on the second floor of the family's house at 83 Beals Street. Delivering your baby at home was common in 1917, as was dying.

My second year of school, I lived in Newton with a college student from Brandeis University, and occasionally house-sat in Sudbury for members of a church where I worked, but it was as part of a prison post-release program where I learned about dying at home. All three years of seminary, I volunteered with the Catholic Chaplaincy team at Walpole Prison (now known as Cedar Junction). The maximum security prison held 800 men— far more than the facility was designed to house. Most were doubled up in 9-by-5-foot cells.

I taught Bible study in the chapel, helped a little with worship, visited the men in the isolation units and staffed a program called "Sesame Street" alongside several inmates who provided childcare for the youngest visitors. Prisons are especially terrifying for children. The physical plant alone is intimidating— observation towers, barbed wire, barred doors and bulletproof glass. Add to that the pat-down procedures and the potential of strip searches and most grown-ups are petrified. The Sesame

Street inmate volunteers calmed the little ones with games and books and art projects. Once when I was anxious about getting an appointment after graduation, one of the men tried to reassure me that things would work out. "Don't you worry," he said. " If the bishop doesn't give you a church, we'll steal you one."

Dot Walsh, a charismatic, middle-aged laywoman who unofficially ran the Catholic team asked me if I would help her open a post-release home for the men. So often prisoners who have served extended sentences outlive or are estranged from their families. Moreover, they are like Rip Van Winkle returning to a familiar place that has changed dramatically in their absence. The home she had in mind was a multi-bedroom, two-story house on the border of Jamaica Plains and Roxbury. I pulled the evening shift four nights a week.

Even before the residents moved into the house, Dot asked me if I would help one man transition out of Norfolk Prison. She explained that he had been granted early release. The prisoner had advanced-stage cancer and the state decided that he could die at home. The problem was that he didn't have a home. Members of Dot's parish agreed to let him stay with them, but the couple couldn't cancel all of their obligations indefinitely. Could I sit with him some afternoons?

Have I mentioned that I faint at the sight of blood, and if you start vomiting, I will too? I was 23 years old and I had never been with someone who was really sick. My grandfather who I wrote about in the introduction died suddenly in Florida when I was in college. He left his body to science, thinking that medical students could learn quite a bit from his cadaver given his history with polio and cancer. I had never even been inside a funeral home.

"OK Dot," I said against my better judgment. Leon was restricted to a hospital bed from the first night I visited. We played chess. We talked about his years of incarceration, his family, his crime. He managed to bring me out of my introverted shell and then, after about a month and a half, he gave me the greatest gift a future pastor could receive: He slipped away peacefully one night while we were alone. "Oh death, where is your sting?" I read at my first funeral and I thought about Leon.

Volunteering involves a reciprocal relationship. You give and you get. We won the volunteer lottery when we got Loren Sohn. He is a member at Orchard United Methodist and I was invited there one night to talk about the possibility of the congregation sponsoring a tiny home. Theirs was the first church to make a major financial commitment. They organized a steering committee and got busy fundraising. Church members sold "shingles" made from shims for $1 apiece (about the cost of a shingle) to use as Christmas tree ornaments or gift tags. Janice Mitchell stitched together a beautiful tiny house quilt that sold for $3,000 at a fundraising auction. They listed-off some house items and had people donate to cover the costs. Loren's wife, Sue, who was active on the committee, paid for a toilet as part of his Christmas gift. All told, the suburban congregation raised enough to sponsor the Cass Victorian home.

Loren had been a project manager at IBM for more than 10 years before he retired and had also

Cass Tiny Homes Volunteer Tasks

- Hang dry wall – plus taping and sanding
- Install Flooring
- Assemble Cabinets and Furniture
- Paint – exterior and interior
- Install base boards, counter tops and tile/back splashes
- Mount towel racks, toilet paper dispensers, shower bars
- Make/hang curtains and blinds
- Prepare the grounds – removing stones, bricks, other trash
- Install sod/seeding
- Handle other landscaping – flowers, bushes, planting additional trees
- Put up fencing
- Clean-up construction debris
- Serve as tour guides

volunteered with Rebuilding Together as a workday organizer. Thus, he possessed the interpersonal skills, construction knowledge and organizational abilities we needed. He loves to give groups a meaningful experience, so he returned countless voicemails and emails. He lined up teams and tasks using a Gantt chart. He volunteered to be on site three days a week. He would jump in and teach people new skills when needed and was willing to watch others who are veteran builders.

Many of the project funders sent work teams: the Ford Fund, the Junior League of Detroit, S.A.Y. Detroit, Home Depot, First Presbyterian Church of Ann Arbor, Birmingham First United Methodist Church, Chelsea First United Methodist Church and St. Kenneth's Catholic Church from Plymouth. The groups provided peoplepower that allowed us to stretch our budget by eliminating labor costs as well as donating extra items as they were needed—paint and paint brushes, gloves, flowers, mulch, etc.

We were very fortunate to have Habituals, too. These adults had years of experience assisting Habitat for Humanity with their builds. Since Habitat Detroit was on a construction hiatus, several teams were eager to volunteer at Cass. Tom Thompson and his Habitat group came faithfully every Wednesday. The men and women brought their own tools and their own lunches (not that they took much time out to eat).

Dave Adams is nearly 80, but could pass for early 60s. His wife, Barb, is one of those people who never stops—and they are a team. We knew immediately that they were highly skilled. When we were in a pinch, Loren called them. They indicated they could join us for a day. After the first day they returned again. Then, they changed their plans to help for a total of seven more days. They nearly single-handedly did the trim in six houses. Volunteers like this are invaluable.

The most demanding job was hanging drywall. Not everyone can or should do this. Plus, it is a multi-day process and, so, it requires teams that can commit a week or so to hang the drywall, tape it, mud it, sand it smooth and prime it before painting. Conversely, painting seems relatively easy—but not everyone can or should paint. We have learned to give instructions about painting ceilings, priming walls and painting with rollers and brushes. We have also resigned ourselves to the fact that no one washes the rollers or brushes when they are finished.

Volunteers installed vinyl plank flooring in the homes. It looks good, is easy to put down and can stand up to liquid spills. There are two types, both of which require supervision by someone who knows what they are doing: interlocking, which takes some finessing; and glue strip (peel and stick), which goes down easily but needs careful placement because it doesn't come up effortlessly once it has been set.

The floors for an entire home can be completed in one day by three or four people. Once done, they need to be covered because work on the rest of the home resumes. We discovered that using flooring protector—heavy paper that goes over the flooring while construction continues—is a must. Fiberock, kraft paper, and Builder Board are some common names. The whole tiny house can be covered for about $30.

On average, volunteers contributed about 350 hours per house. That is 50 hours per week for seven weeks (about the time it took us to finish the interiors). Realistically, you cannot have more than four people in a house at a time, otherwise they are bumping into each other and it presents a safety hazard.

There were some takeaways with the first set of homes in relation to volunteer tasks:

- Flat-pack cabinets required "some" assembly, which took much longer than we anticipated. Volunteers who can install cabinets rarely like to assemble cabinets!
- Hang the uppers first while you have easy access.
- Make sure the cabinets are level. It's essential to supporting the countertop.
- You need a pro or someone with significant experience to install the countertops.
- Make sure you get touch-up paint. The cabinets will inevitably get bumped.

- Estimate one day to assemble and install cabinets. Our kitchens only used four to six cabinets.
- Pre-paint the trim, interior doors, baseboard moldings, window moldings, etc. with interior semi-gloss.
- Use a nail gun.
- Spackle the nail holes, do not caulk the nail holes.
- Caulk the top of the baseboard and around the windows, if needed.

Two other volunteers should be mentioned. Jeff Lockledge, Ph.D., a former computer programming professor and current senior director at Sirius XM, used his laptop to handle all the logistics for the development early on. He surfed the Web and sourced materials and appliances, ensuring that thrift was built into our budget. Jeff, a member of the Nardin Park UMC, helped fundraise and friend-raise, too. He was the one who recruited Richard Scheck and his network of architectural and construction connections.

Designer Deb Hollis also played a crucial role. She owns Interior Lifestyles and helped us select colors, patterns, furniture and wall decorations. Deb turned the indistinguishable conformity of affordable housing on its head so that each home had a theme carried out in accent walls and cozy bedrooms, amazing kitchens with delicious tile backsplashes, eye-catching lamps and clocks and art work. After the first seven homes were complete, we held a Tiny Homes Progressive Tour (which included a catered meal with a different dish in each home) during the Memorial Day weekend. Five hundred people paid generously to see the homes and the feedback was overwhelmingly positive. The guests couldn't stop talking about how beautifully they were decorated.

Ford Motor Company sent volunteer teams of employees day after day to tackle a number of projects. Photo used with the permission of the Ford Fund.

Left: The Albion College Fellows filled dumpsters with unearthed garbage and construction debris. In addition to corporate, scout and student groups, teams came from numerous churches. Right: Members of Brighton First United Methodist Church climbed about 20 feet up to install drywall in the Junior League house. Loren Sohn is half hidden by the scaffolding.

Andrew ▓▓▓▓ Homeless Veterans, the low income elderly absolutely! All of the bums, and junkies hell no! There should be a list of strict qualifications; in order to be approved. However we're talking about Detroit here! Those idiots can't even tie their shoes! It will be a total failure!
Like · Reply · September 14, 2016 at 12:46am · Edited

Gino ▓▓▓▓ homeless people will not be able to afford these! the rent is a dollar a sq ft. so if you have a 400 sq. foot close house that's $400 a month + utilites, groceries etc. they don't have jobs what makes you think they can afford a mortgage
Like · Reply · September 15, 2016 at 9:58am

Wesley ▓▓▓▓ A place for them to shoot up their drugs. I watched drugs Inc. Most of these homeless people in Detroit have a serious crack addiction or meth problem. I have a better solution for em. Give him a drug test if they fail put them on a boat take them a couple miles out to Lake Michigan and throw him overboard
Like · Reply · September 15, 2016 at 12:46pm

Mitcheal ▓▓▓▓ Why do those motherf▓▓▓rs need a house when they have no f▓▓ing job
Like · Reply · September 15, 2016 at 11:27pm

Jean ▓▓▓▓ love the idea of students and the elderly. Awesome project. Didn't mean to sound so negative.
Like · Reply · September 16, 2016 at 9:11pm

Rhonda ▓▓▓▓ hard working single ....divorced victim of domestic violence and I can't get a drop of help because I have a "good" job making just over 10.00 per hour
Like · Reply · September 17, 2016 at 8:44pm

Ryan ▓▓▓▓ Now they will have a roof over there head when they do crack 😈
Like · Reply · September 18, 2016 at 10:46am

Marcia ▓▓▓▓ Wow some of you are so judgemental. I am handicapped. I have worked hard all my life. I am living in a weekly rental motel and so close to the edge of being homeless. There is a 3 year wait for housing. It took almost 3 years to get social security. I had to go without medical care for those three years. I begged and borrow. My current housing in the motel is horrendous. It's run down and I fear that a storm will send concrete smashing or me. One rooms ceiling has already fallen in. I am one of the lucky ones. I have a roof over my head. There are a shocking amount of elderly and handicapped living here. So get up on your high horse and explain how we don't deserve safe clean housing.
Like · Reply · September 19, 2016 at 11:24am

12

Residential Diversity

FORTUNATELY, IT WASN'T necessary to steal a church. I was sent to one on the west side of Detroit: William S. Ford Memorial Church. (United Methodist pastors are appointed and they are itinerant, meaning they move within a geographic area at the pleasure of the resident bishop and the district superintendents who work with him/her.) It was the first time in my life that I lived in a house that didn't belong to my parents. I loved that it had a fireplace. One night I had the flames going so hot that the fireplace glass doors exploded. I was also ecstatic that I could finally own a dog. Luckily, my pup wasn't in close proximity to the doors when they burst.

The parsonage (a house owned by the church) was located directly across the street from the church. I would have preferred another location for privacy's sake, but I grew to appreciate that it was in the middle of a very diverse neighborhood. There was a strong Roman Catholic/Polish presence. Most of the elementary-aged children attended St. Christopher School. The seniors walked to daily Mass in the early mornings, and the Polish Catholic homeowners kept immaculate lawns and were seriously committed to the neighborhood CB patrol. Once or twice a month I would ride shotgun with someone from St. Christopher's Parish as part of the community watch. We would take breaks at the bakeries and restaurants on the commercial strip, which served incredible cabbage soup and *pierogi*.

African-American households were newer and fewer in the community. They comprised about one-fourth of the area even though they represented a majority of the city as a whole. Black people made up most of the households living in the Herman Gardens housing project, located half a mile north of the parsonage between Tireman Street and Joy Road east of the Southfield Freeway. Built in the 1940s, the brick buildings had experienced deferred maintenance inside and out. At one point, the city moved homeless individuals into some of the vacant units. I remember hauling up beds, sofas and dining room sets for the new residents who were "relocated" without furniture, food, dishes or a support network.

The African-Americans who lived in the houses and apartments near me were mostly middle class. Although Ford Memorial UMC only had two black families who regularly attended, we started an eight-week summer program that provided education, recreation and field trips for 150 elementary-aged kids, about half of which were African-American. We converted the basement of the parsonage into a computer lab. Eight rented PCs were hooked up around the furnace, hot water heater and laundry machines. The teachers had to pry children off the keyboards at the end of each session. Oregon Trail was the game of choice.

Finally, people from the Middle East peppered the blocks surrounding the church. The neighborhood was pocketed by Dearborn. So many Arab Americans lived in the suburb at that time that it was considered their unofficial capital. Long before the media was talking about "sleeper cells," "radicalized" individuals and "no-fly" lists, I realized that I knew next to nothing about Islam or the cultural and political geography of Iran, Iraq, Syria, Saudi Arabia and Qatar. Over time, I was introduced to a few imams, interacted with men wearing a *kaffiyeh* headdress, met women wearing their *hijab* and was invited to attend ecumenical events in the mosque on Ford Road. My knowledge was still relatively superficial when the United States began bombing Kuwait in 1991 in an attempt to expel Iraqi troops. To the rest of the nation, the nonstop aerial images on CNN may have looked like the video games our students played in the parsonage basement—but it took on a totally different dimension for me as I reflected on what the war meant to my neighbors.

More and more local businesses were purchased by people who installed signs with Arabic lettering rather than English. As far as businesses go, there were 13 drinking establishments within a mile of the parsonage including Gigi's, a gay bar. Patrons entered the windowless building from the parking lot in back to avoid confrontations with agitators. Conversely, the pornographic bookstore at the corner of W. Warren Avenue and Greenfield Road, half a mile east of the parsonage, forced customers to park in back and walk on the sidewalk to the front of the store to enter. The main street also included Dr. Faye's veterinary, a Dairy Queen, a motorcycle club, a karate school, Eddie's Florist, a used-car lot that never appeared to have customers, a funeral home that advertised cheap prices for cremations and a grocery store which utilized yellow cement poles at the doors to keep people from stealing the shopping carts.

Higher crime rates can be one of the tradeoffs of urban life, but diversity is one of the rewards of living in a big city. When planning Cass Tiny Homes, we felt it was essential to include residents with a variety of ages and experiences. What's more, we didn't want outsiders stereotyping the development as "where the homeless live." Therefore, it was determined to include three groups of people for the home ownership program: formerly homeless men and women; young adults who had aged-out of foster care; and low-income senior citizens.

The formerly homeless individuals or couples will occupy at least half of the 25 tiny homes. These applicants had to have a regular income, and so most don't come directly off the street. Rather, they applied from shelters and housing programs. Some were living in one of Cass' residential facilities, but they also originated from other agencies. Some have been shuffling between friends and relatives. Critics regularly argued that we should narrow the pool to only homeless veterans. Although Cass already does house veterans, thanks to increased federal funding, there are far fewer homeless vets today in Michigan.[38]

The remainder of the homes will be divided. A handful are reserved for **young adults who have aged-out of foster care** at age 18 or 21. (In Michigan, there is a program called Young Adult Voluntary Foster Care which extends services until recipients reach 21 if they sign-up for it). At either age, they frequently lack the adult and financial support to begin the next phase of their lives. The majority of this group has been living with foster families for years. A number of them have been juggled between more than five foster homes. Thus, they stand to benefit from both the community resources of the Tiny Homes and the financial opportunities that the development provides.

Low-income senior citizens will also rent-to-own the homes. Elderly people are typically waitlisted for affordable housing in Detroit. It is common for them to remain on the list for three years or more. Some of these seniors linger in houses

> # Statistics about Aging Out *from the Annie E. Casey Foundation*
>
> - Only 58% graduate from high school by age 19 (compared with 87% of all 19-year-olds)
> - More than 20% will become homeless
> - Within two years of leaving the foster care system, 25% will be involved with the justice system
> - About 70% of young women become pregnant by 21
> - At the age of 24, only half are employed[39]

that they have occupied for decades but are no longer able to physically or financially maintain. Others have been forced out of apartments and neighborhoods that were being gentrified. The single story, limited space of the Tiny Homes is ideal for folks who have physical restrictions.

Henri Nouwen co-authored a book about the elderly with Walter J. Gaffney called *Aging: The Fulfillment of Life*.[40] It opens with an old Balinese legend about a remote mountain village. The cautionary tale explains that the people of the village sacrificed and ate the old men so that there came a time when not a single male senior remained. Consequently, the area traditions were lost.

Some time thereafter, the village wanted to build an assembly hall. But when the builders inspected the trees that had been cut down, they were unable to determine the tops of the trunks from the bottoms. This was a major problem because if the lumber was positioned the wrong way, the structure could cave in upon itself.

A young man approached the assembly and said that if the village promised to never kill and eat the old men again, he could solve their dilemma. They promised, and the young man retrieved his grandfather, whom he had hidden away. Then, the legend concludes, the old man taught the community to tell the tops from the bottoms.

Rather than thinking of the elderly, the homeless or young people who have aged-out of foster care as a problem—segregating them, ostracizing them, expelling them or excommunicating

Above: A restaurant and bakery/market near my first church on Detroit's west side.

them—we decided that they could be teachers to each other and to us. The elders could help younger adults learn about tradition and how to deal with loss. The 20-somethings could remind their neighbors to change the things they cannot accept and to hope against hope. The middle-aged folks who had been homeless could educate some to take safety precautions and to practice gratitude.

A few Cass staff members applied for the program. As long as they met the income guidelines and fit into the formerly homeless, senior citizen and/or foster care categories, they were deemed eligible for consideration.

The first group of tiny homes residents ranged in age from age 24 to 74. All but one resident was a person of color. The average income was $988 a month, slightly less than $12,000 a year. Only one person had ever owned a home before.

13

Applications and Screening Process

DUE TO THE intense media coverage, we decided to distribute applications in October 2016. Years of running permanent supportive housing meant that we knew what could, should and were forbidden to be included in the document. Applications were distributed from the Scott Building security booth. Interested individuals had to show up in person to request an application. We wanted folks to have to make the effort, and we thought they should see the neighborhood in which the homes would be built. There was some negative feedback from people who deemed the process unreasonable.

October 23

Its really not fair that you would not have a downloadable form on your site for everyone in America to have the opportunity to apply. I have a crappy life in the west and there's no way I can get to MI to get an app and return it! So much for something great going on there!
(Sent from OUTLOOK)

Anais@Applications and Screening Process

Others disapproved because we wouldn't provide all of the information for them to build our Tiny Homes in their respective locations.

Hello.

My name is Oleg. I live in Russia.

I saw your mini at home and I really liked it. Want to build yourself a house. Could you send me a photo or video inside the house, or sketches or project. I house very much, but I have no money to buy a full project. Help me please to build your dream home. Build will be of brick, size 20x20x40 santimeters. Thank you.

--

С Уважением

Nevertheless, by October 31, 2016, 122 people had completed and submitted applications. From November 1 through May 1, 2017, over 900 additional people requested an application. Interestingly enough, when considering the business plan, one of our board members asked if we really thought anyone would want to live in a tiny home. A committee was formed to handle screening. Since there were nearly five applications for every home, the group determined disqualifiers before they even opened one of the sealed envelopes. The factors of elimination were:

- **Incomplete applications.** The application instructions made it clear that all questions must be answered, and that all attachments must be enclosed. Several applications did not qualify because the prospective person didn't include the required references.

- **Is currently living outside Michigan.** Given that we were only proposing to build 25 homes, it made sense to focus on people already living in Michigan. This saddened a good number of people who offered to relocate from California, Florida, Pennsylvania, Texas, etc. We also received a compelling letter from London:

Dear who it may concern,

I am writing to you on behalf of myself and my partner. I would like to know if you can make a Xmas dream come true for us in 2017.

4 weeks before Xmas my partner went to his door to answer the bell, and some guys said they wanted to come in. My partner said, "no, you cannot come in."

So they set about him. They punched him in the eye, hit him over the head with a fire extinguisher and kicked him about the floor. And on top of that, his Landlord wanted to take his house away by February 2017 which will leave him homeless.

Me and him had difficult times so I left and found my own place. Things is getting better between us and we hoped to be together again one day. I saw in a magazine your lovely little houses being constructed with your Cass Community Social Services in Detroit and thought how nice if me and George and his dog could start a new life together in one of those little houses.

I am a pro singer and George is an Electrical Engineer (qualified). George will not go anywhere without his beloved dog. As I said, his home is soon to be taken away. He has not had hot water for 8 weeks. His ceiling leeks. It is in a very bad way. It would be great if you could make this wish come true – not so much for me but for the man I love so much.

Yours hopeing, K.W.

The Christmas miracle was that the note was delivered even though it was addressed to the Cass Community Social Services, Detroit, MI 48201 (without a street address and the wrong zip code).

- **A conviction(s) of violence within the last 10 years.** We believe that people can change, but given the number of vulnerable people in our community, we thought it best to have a recent record of nonviolence.
- **Any conviction of a sexual offense.** Again, given the large number of adults with mental illness and the people coming from domestic violence situations (as well as its close proximity of the young people who live or volunteer in the thousands at Cass), we decided to be a sanctuary community. This is not to say that we believe people with sex-crime convictions don't deserve a welcoming community, we just knew that we couldn't be all things to all people.
- **A conviction for selling drugs in the last five years.** Illegal drug activity breeds violence.

Twenty-two applications were disqualified before the second phase began. Next, the committee established a numerical scoring system for ranking the candidates. It was applied to the applicants without identifying names. The four scored items were:

1. **A criminal record.** If yes, what was the nature of his/her conviction? How long ago did it occur and how long has the person been off probation? The committee also elected to use a national screening service so as not to miss a serious conviction in another state.
2. **Residential history.** Did the person's housing history indicate that he/she was ready for housing stability? Were the landlord references positive? If the person had been evicted, how long ago did it occur?
3. **Financial readiness.** Did the individual make at least $9,000 annually? Was the source of income secure? Did he or she have the ability to turn on the electricity?
4. **Personal references.** Did the person's references describe him/her in positive terms? Were the

references independent and unrelated by blood or marriage?

The top scorers were invited in for personal interviews. In addition to getting to know the applicants, the interviews gave staff the opportunity to explain the program expectations. We reviewed the classroom obligations, financial coaching and the volunteer responsibilities to make sure they were aware of these and agreed to them. Then, we explained the "fishbowl" element to the Tiny Homes. Throughout the construction phase, inquisitive people would stop by to see the homes. Some took videos as their cars rolled by. Others got out and posed for selfies on the front lawns. Many trampled the flowers and bushes in order to peer through the windows. We knew that this would continue after people moved into their homes. Thus, we stressed that residents had the right to tell strangers that coming inside their homes was off-limits. But we wanted to make sure they would be all right with having their property photographed. The interviewee was then given a numerical grade.

Applications were ranked by their cumulative score. The highest number was allowed to select the home he/she wanted from the six available. (We build them six at a time.) The second highest score picked from the five remaining. The sixth score had the option of taking the last house or waiting for the next round, in which case we moved on to the seventh highest score. We had anticipated that there may be a couple of wrinkles. For instance, if someone's income only allowed him or her a 250-square-foot house because they made $750 a month, we contended with that up front. Similarly, if an individual had a physical handicap, he/she took priority for the ADA-compliant home.

Curious neighbors and visitors regularly drive by to make videos and take pictures. Many approach the homes and peer inside to get a look of the interior layouts and decorations. For this reason, we decided to keep the first "model" home vacant for months. Tours were offered twice a week for people who were interested. It was thrilling to witness the response of visitors.

Vern ███████ Good idea, however a home is only as good as you take care of it. There needs to be a Mantainance plan worked into the sale as well, or they will be right back where they started, but with a bunch of little shacks

Like · Reply · January 1, 2017 at 9:15am

Matt ███████ Who is going to cut their grass? Trim their landscaping? Clean the siding and gutters when they get dirty in 2 years? If not, you'll just have a tiny house slum.

Like · Reply · September 20, 2016 at 12:54pm

Janette ███████ Great idea. From homeless to home owner. Now that's the way to solve a problem. 👎

Like · Reply · September 15, 2016 at 12:54pm

Donna ███████ All about the project , but in Michigan they Love to charge high property tax, and also Detroit has a water bill each person must pay. Going into the program please make sure the will not lose home to taxes. ....

Like · Reply · September 16, 2016 at 1:29pm

14

Educational Components of the Program

FOR 10 YEARS, I owned an investment property—I was a landlord. Primarily, the experience taught me how to repair things on a shoestring budget—garbage disposals, toilet guts, lawnmower blades and broken windows. Beyond that, the experience taught me about people. I learned, for instance, that prospective tenants could give you a favorable impression on paper and in person hide the fact that they were dysfunctional, sociopathic individuals with horrible hygiene deficits. What's more, renters in one of my units moved in a friend without my permission who was struggling with some personal issues. There were signs right away—like the fact that he spray-painted graffiti inside the duplex. One night after 11 p.m., I looked out my kitchen window to see that he was having what seemed to be an "Eyes Wide Shut" party in our shared backyard. What caused me to look out? A 40-piece marching band had surrounded the pool and was playing dirge-style music. Two days later when I ran into him, I asked about the event. He responded nonchalantly that they had come to perform for his cat's funeral. It turns out he had buried the feline in the backyard.

Generally people want to be good tenants. Sometimes they lack the knowledge that owners have acquired over time. How do you respond when water is backing up in the basement? Is the reason you don't have hot water because the pilot light went out? What size is your furnace filter and how often does it need to be changed? Good renters call the landlord when they notice a problem. Property owners don't have that luxury and so, since most of the Tiny Homes' residents will be first-time homeowners, we elected to make a monthly homeownership class part of the residential program. It deals with cleaning processes and products, preventative maintenance, seasonal upkeep requirements, "handyperson" skills and using a contractor.

Here is the Homeownership 101 syllabus:

1. **Cleaning Processes and Products**

   Floors—laminate and tile

   Windows and mirrors

   Countertops (including granite)

   Front-load washers and dryers (including removing lint)

   Refrigerators/freezers (including defrosting)

   Stoves (including how to remove grease from and around the stovetop)

   Microwaves

   Bathroom sinks, shower/tubs and toilets

   Kitchen sinks

2. **Maintaining a Toolbox and/or Borrowing Tools**

   What tools to acquire and where to buy them inexpensively

   How to use them

   Safety measures

   What tools are available for loan from the Cass warehouse

3. **Preventative Maintenance**

   Spring—check roof, siding/wood for damage, interior painting

   Summer—AC checkup, exterior painting, landscaping chores

   Fall—leaf removal/gutters, furnace filter supply

   Winter—use of salt/snow removal, what to do if there is a power outage.

4. **Basic Handyperson**

   Electrical—fuse box, light fixture replacement, energy-efficient light bulb disposal

   Plumbing—toilets, sinks, shower/tubs (What to do when the drain/toilet is clogged. How to fix a toilet chain. What to use to stop a leak. Hair and drains don't mix)

   Drywall repair

   Painting—drop cloths, outlet covers, scraping/sanding, spackle, clean walls/surfaces, taping, the differences between primer, interior and exterior paints, water-based or oil-based paints, Rust-Oleum, Kilz, etc.

   Removal and replacement of flooring or tiles

5. **Security System and Crime Prevention**
6. **Pest Control**

   Mice, rats, ants, cockroaches, bedbugs, bees, etc.

7. **Household Emergencies**

   What to do if an animal gets in the home, the heat is out, etc.

8. **Independent Contractors**—get bids, check references, make sure they have adequate insurance; partial payments upfront

   Carpenter

   Electrician

PTAC, HVAC—heating and cooling

Plumber

Roofer

Security system repair

Window repairs/replacements

9. **Landscaping and Lawn Maintenance**

10. **Trash and Recycling**

11. **Understanding the Schedule for Property Taxes and Homeowners Insurance** (including what to look for in selecting an insurance provider and policy).

12. **Recordkeeping**

Organizing receipts and records of repairs as well as instructional manuals (what can be saved electronically to maximize storage)

Since none of the houses have garages, we decided to establish a tool warehouse across the street from the Tiny Homes. Residents have access to a number of common tools such as a lawnmower, rake, edger, clippers, shovel, paint brush, pan, roller, ladder, etc. This eliminated the need to store or buy larger items. Like Uber and Airbnb, sharing makes economic sense. The procedure is the same one that the agency uses for the Cass Bike Bank. A borrower simply leaves a photo identification until he/she is done with the item and it is given back to him/her once the loaned equipment is returned.

Lastly, the homeownership classes help people adjust to living in a smaller space. Some residents, especially the seniors just moving in, required downsizing. All the furniture from a larger apartment or house does not fit into a tiny home. (Furniture is made available at no charge for individuals who need something or everything.) During the classes, teachers offer suggestions about organizing books, dishes and clothing. Michigan's seasons require apparel for 5 degrees and 90 degrees. The class discusses how to streamline a closet and how to craft storage cubbies under their beds, on top of walls, inside footstools and on shelves. A tiny home is no place for a hoarder.

The homeowners' classes also provide a great outlet to reinforce good neighbor practices and to review the rental rules about quiet hours, subletters, parking spaces, vaccinating pets and walking dogs on a leash. Furthermore, they allowed residents to make announcements concerning community meetings, trips and campus resources. Are there new residents? Will there be a special meal for the holidays? How about annual inspection dates and times? Do you want to sign up for transportation to the grocery store? All of these types of questions are addressed at the monthly sessions.

Finally, since construction occurred in stages, the residents provided us with valuable feedback. For instance, our homes don't include doorbells because residents can hear guests knocking at the front door. During one homeowners meeting, the men and women requested peepholes so they could determine who was on the porch prior to opening the door. Now every house that doesn't have a large window in the door includes a swivel peephole with the flange on the inside and a privacy latch. We added steel jams enforcements to the doors, too. During another group meeting, a resident shared that he couldn't punch in the security code on the keypad fast enough to arm and disarm his alarm system due to shaking hands. We purchased a key fob for him to use. The wireless remote reduced the procedure to the a touch of one button.

The second component that residents need to participate in is financial coaching. These sessions are personal rather than communal because the renters are at different financial levels. Some were already religiously squirreling away money for emergencies. Some had been earning extra income for years doing hair or cutting grass. Many low-income individuals are quite resourceful, keeping costs down because they only have small amounts of money. For instance, I had never heard of seven-day car insurance until I started at Cass. In order to renew your license in Michigan, drivers have to provide the Secretary of State proof of auto insurance. As previously mentioned, insurance coverage in Detroit is extremely expensive. Thus, poor people purchase weeklong auto policies for a fraction of what six-month coverage would demand. They then use the documentation to get a license and immediately let the short-term policy lapse. They have calculated that paying a police-issued ticket or two will cost less than obtaining traditional insurance coverage. It's a problem, of course, having up to half of the city drivers uninsured—but it is a real reminder that often people with limited means aren't financially illiterate, they are inventive enough to figure out ways to exist while living in poverty.

Employees from Flagstar Bank volunteered to serve as coaches. They each made a one-year commitment to work with one person/couple. Depending on where their mentee(s) were at the start, the personal sessions generally include the following goals:

- To establish a budget
- To eliminate personal debt
- To repair credit and monitor credit (FICO) score
- To earn additional income
- To open and contribute to a savings account
- To establish a checking account
- To explore investments—make your money work for you
- To plan for retirement
- To avoid predatory lending—payday advances, pawn shops, loan sharks

It is worth noting that the Cass Tiny Homes program is different than other low-income housing projects because earning more income is encouraged. Other programs disincentivize making additional money by increasing rents. (In most affordable housing, rent is based on one-third of the tenant's income. If their income climbs, the rental rate is raised. If their income increases too much, they may be expelled from their housing. Consequently, many people either don't look for opportunities to boost their income or they search for ways to make cash "under the table" so they don't need to declare it.) Cass Tiny Homes will not hoist a resident's rent because it is based on square footage.

If, however, someone's income drops/stops so that the person becomes unable to pay rent even after the staff has intervened, the resident can be evicted during the first seven years. There is no way to keep a house without a small amount of income.

The seven-year rental period provides an extended period of time for the renter to develop both financial discipline and a financial cushion. During that time, Cass acts as the landlord and uses the tenant's money to pay for the person's general living expenses. Our business plan established that the amount paid will adequately cover these essential bills. It is meant to be a break-even proposition. As long as the resident pays the proper amount of rent on time, he/she is demonstrating that they can handle the bills. When the tenant takes over the house, they will stop

Above: A photo of one of the spray-painted walls that my troubled tenant contributed to my investment property. This was in the kitchen.

paying rent and begin assuming the payments that the nonprofit had been handling. There is no mortgage.

The only bill beyond rent, which is the resident's responsibility during the rental period, is electricity (which includes heat). The average amount of this runs $20 a month thanks to the energy efficiency of the homes and their small sizes. During the coldest winter months, both heat and electric should be less than $35. As part of the home-ownership classes, residents will be reminded of ways to reduce electricity demands.

Lastly, some have been critical of the program because it doesn't require "sweat equity" in the way that Habitat for Humanity does. Habitat has a good model. Homeowners contribute time during the build with the volunteer crews, and some affiliates have future owners do other things such as volunteer at the ReStore shops. The thought is that they will acquire building and repair skills during the process and that they will value their homes that much more.

Ours is just a different model. Cass Tiny Homes' residents pick up the handyperson skills in the classes while they are renters. This way they get to know their neighbors and together they review how to handle problems/preventative maintenance as situations occur. The residents are also expected to volunteer. Their time commitment is a minimum of eight hours a month for seven years (or approximately 680 hours). For instance some volunteer to staff shifts with the community watch. Every resident "patrols" in a car with another community member and monitors the neighborhood each month. The pair looks for stolen vehicles, illegal drug activity, anyone breaking into a house, as well as watching for a neighbor who might be in trouble as evidenced by things such as overflowing mail or snow left unshoveled.

By participating in the community watch, the residents will become acquainted with their neighbors and familiar with their surroundings, help identify community problems/solutions and, potentially, discourage criminal activity. (They are not allowed to carry weapons while volunteering and they are not permitted to stop criminals. Instead, the volunteers notify Cass security and/or the police about their observations.) Their involvement in the watch will help community members know the Tiny Homes' residents and appreciate their contribution to the larger neighborhood. Moreover, this citizen engagement program can potentially impact property values. Prospective buyers everywhere are concerned about safety.

$aving and Compounding

IF YOU STARTED SAVING $12 A PAYCHECK
(OR $300 A YEAR) AT AGE 25 FOR 50 YEARS...

and you put your money under your mattress at
0% interest – you would have $15,000

or you deposited it in a savings account with
3% interest - you would have $35,000

or you socked it away in a 401 (k)/403 (b) with
9% interest - you would have $280,000

or you invested it in stocks which made
12% interest - you would have $1,050,000

THE GOAL IS TO START EARLY
(TODAY IF YOU HAVEN'T STARTED YET)
AND MAKE YOUR MONEY WORK FOR YOU.

Suzanne ▓▓▓▓ Separate homes like this would be hard to oversee. Will someone be checking these places regularly to ensure they aren't getting trashed or becoming crack houses?
Like · Reply · September 14, 2016 at 7:20am

Sailor ▓▓▓▓ God bless america 👍 ❤️ 🇺🇸
Like · Reply · September 14, 2016 at 11:11pm

Arnell ▓▓▓▓ Grate idea
Like · Reply · September 14, 2016 at 11:47pm

Judy ▓▓▓▓ This will only work if you have someone in charge to help the people take care of their property and set guidelines. Seems like you would have to create private security too! Its not getting a home that is the problem. Its teaching people to take care of themselves and their property. Great concept! I hope it works! Seems like people will have to through an extensive drug, alcohol and mental rehab to obtain one of these homes.
Like · Reply · February 1, 2017 at 11:03am · Edited

Frank ▓▓▓▓ This is better than hud because the people will own it and thats what makes a difference
Like · Reply · March 3, 2017 at 10:49am

15

Governance

WHEN I WAS 40 years old, the housing policy for United Methodist pastors in Michigan changed—I no longer had to live in a church-owned parsonage. I could finally buy a home. I decided on one in Corktown, Detroit's oldest surviving neighborhood. The original farms in the area were divided in the 1830s and—because immigrants from Cork County, Ireland were pouring into the region—the neighborhood was named to reflect its emergent population. By the end of the Civil War, Germans (both Catholic and Protestant) were also moving into the district. Most of the people occupied simple frame houses. Wood buildings were common at that time because Michigan had an abundant supply of lumber. Almost all the residents were working-class people.[41]

In 1849, a worker's row house was built on Corktown's Sixth Street to accommodate the increasing number of immigrants.[42] The 3,560-square-foot structure offered three two-story units that weren't much smaller than the detached shotgun houses going up nearby. The difference was that many more occupants were crammed into the row house. As with my seminary apartment, not everyone was there at the same time. Adults alternated shifts sleeping and working. There were few amenities available, but residents accessed help from Most Holy Trinity Church, which stood immediately to the south.

Given that the building has been vacant since the 1980s, it is a small miracle that it wasn't razed as part of the demolition required for parking lots or freeway construction. Nearly three-quarters of the original neighborhood has been torn down.[43] The row house is currently owned by the Greater Corktown Development Corporation. The nonprofit group plans to restore the no-frills facility to use as a museum that will depict the lives of immigrant families from 1840 to the present time. Fortunately, thousands of artifacts have been unearthed on the property. Staff and students from Wayne State University have conducted several archeological digs. Period pottery, pipes, hairbrushes and silverware will be displayed.

Although many local, longtime residents may not be aware of the row house, Corktown is well known for "the Corner"—the northwest corner of Michigan and Trumbull that was home to professional baseball for over 100 years. The wooden Bennett Park stadium was erected on the corner in 1896. A concrete and steel baseball park called Navin Field replaced the wobbly ballpark in April 1912. In 1939, Navin Field was expanded and re-named Briggs Stadium. Then in 1961, the name was changed to Tiger Stadium, after the team. Parents and their baseball mitt-clad children cheered for the greatest hometown players: Ty Cobb, Hank Greenberg, Al Kaline, Willie Horton, Kirk Gibson, Cecil Fielder and more from the boxes and the bleachers. They also applauded visiting greats like Babe Ruth and Ted Williams. After the Detroit rebellion/riots in 1967, the Tigers won the 1968 World Series, which helped heal some of the city's open wounds. (I used 2 words to depict what happened in 1967 because there remains a deep division along racial lines about the cause of the unrest and what term depicts what happened. African-Americans mainly refer to it as a "rebellion" or an "uprising" while white people generally call it a "riot.")

For those who didn't enjoy the national pastime, the stadium on the Corner was an impressive venue for other events. Pat Boone, Kiss and the Eagles all performed there. Fighter Joe Louis defended his heavyweight title against Bob Pastor there in front of a crowd of 33,686. Thousands looking for inspiration joined Billy Graham's crusade congregation and thousands more showed up for the Nelson Mandela stadium rally after he was released from a South African prison. The Detroit Police and Fire departments hosted annual "field day" fundraisers at the Corner. What's more, from 1938 until 1974, the Detroit Lions took to the gridiron there. The football team was wooed away to the Pontiac Silverdome with its artificial turf, 82,000 unobstructed seats, ample corporate suites and 127 acres including a gigantic paved parking lot that encircled the arena.

When the Detroit Tigers vacated the stadium in 2000 to move to Comerica Park downtown, it was controversial. There was a campaign to keep the baseball team at the Corner or at least to save the historic structure. Just a few blocks east sits the deserted Michigan Central Station. The two colossal abandoned buildings stood like neighborhood bookends and there were dire predictions about the future of Corktown. Indeed, the majority of the restaurants, bars and parking lots drew the bulk of their customers from the stadium attendees.

I purchased my home in Corktown during the last season at the old ballpark. An idea came to me during the summer: Since the new house was within walking distance and everyone was projecting a capacity crowd for the final game, I thought it would be good to ask a suburban pastor if he would like to use my driveway that afternoon. Bill Ritter was an avid Tigers' fan, and over the years he had done scores of favors for Cass. Finally, I could thank him in a tangible way. He accepted. On September 27, 1999, I was at school and Bill arrived to park using his reserved spot, only to discover that there were nine vehicles solidly packed on my driveway, tripled up from the fence to the sidewalk. Bill was forced to frantically locate a substitute spot.

I was unaware of the situation until I returned from class, at which point I couldn't even park next to my own house.

Wedging my car to block the driveway apron, I had a long, loud, colorful conversation with myself about the freeloaders who had parked on my property. At last, the ninth inning was over and the scoreboard was shut off. Motorists returned to my street to retrieve their cars.

"Who gave you permission to use my driveway?" I verbally attacked the first man to approach a vehicle behind my blockade.

"I paid $30 to park here," he snapped back.

"To whom? I own the property," I said not knowing if he was telling the truth.

He pointed without hesitation to the house next door. All of the other vehicle owners would orally repeat the same answer. One of my new neighbors was a teenager. Evidently, he had rented out my driveway by selling spots to the sports fans, and pocketed the cash. I confronted his mother once all the cars were gone. She defended her child by saying he would never do such a thing. "All those people are lying on him." I didn't ask her if she volunteered with the welcome wagon.

Despite the cool relationship with the neighbors, my new old Victorian house was wonderful. Built in 1864 by Prussian carpenter Joseph H. Esterling, it was loaded with character and charming features. It had 9-foot ceilings beautifully framed with crown molding. There were some original wide-plank wood floors, five-panel Victorian doors with white porcelain doorknobs and a woodburning stove. The downstairs bathroom had a deep claw-foot tub next to a small marble sink. The Italianate-style exterior was equally impressive. The face of house was distinguished with rounded panes of glass on a bay window, elaborate window heads and elongated columns on the front porch. Though, like the house on Eleven Mile in Royal Oak, there are no level floors and it was totally devoid of insulation.

What I really didn't appreciate until after I purchased the house was that its historic designation would make refurbishing it complicated. There were so many rules. Any work on the exterior would require the approval of the Detroit Historic Commission: Window replacement; gutter replacement; roof replacement; landscaping changes; porch repairs; fence installation; paint colors; even changes to the back side of the house, not visible from the street, required permission to proceed.

The rules for the Tiny Homes' renters are similar. Any outside alterations need advance approval. Interior cosmetic changes do not. During the seven-year rental period, leases regulate what tenants can and cannot do:

- **Acceptable Additions** – Renters cannot increase square footage of the home. Nor can they build a shed or garage without advance approval.

- **Alcohol and Drugs** – Renters are not permitted to manufacture or sell intoxicating liquor or grow, manufacture or sell illegal drugs. Renters who use medically prescribed marijuana must provide documentation.

- **Conducting a Business** – Renters can utilize their home for legal business purposes with advance approval.

- **Decorations** – Renters are limited to the types of decorations they can put on the homes and the length of time they can leave the decorations up.

- **Fencing and Hedges** – Renters are prohibited from removing or adding fencing to the property. Likewise, they may not plant hedges or trees to obstruct the view of their home or yard.

- **Inspections** – Renters shall grant city of Detroit employees permission to enter their home annually for inspection purposes. If repairs are needed, they must allow Cass staff or contractors access in a timely manner so the home will remain compliant as a rental property.

- **Liquid Furniture** – Waterbeds are not permitted.

- **Parking** – Renters can park their cars on the street or in a garage. Vehicles are not allowed on the front or back lawns.

- **Pets** – Renters may have up to two pets (dogs, cats) as long as the animal(s) weigh 50 pounds or less and there is proof of licensing.
- **Pools and Hot Tubs** – Pools and hot tubs are not permitted.
- **Possession of Weapons, Fireworks, etc.** – Renters are not permitted to keep any type of gun unless they provide documentation that it is required for a job and it is properly licensed. They are not allowed to keep or use fireworks on the property.
- **Renting to Others or Subletting** – Renters may not rent or sublet their homes.
- **Yards** – Renters shall insure that the lawn is cut and the snow is removed.

During the rental years, a homeowners association (HOA) is expected to be established. We will retain legal counsel to work with the renters and a representative staff member to create the appropriate documents such as Articles of Incorporation and Bylaws. In addition to outlining the size and structure of the board, officers' terms and responsibilities, the number of meetings, etc., the responsibility for rules and regulations will be shifted to the new organization incrementally. The documents will also establish written policies for conflicts of interest, whistleblowers, an independent audit, fundraising, gift acceptance, donor intent and donor privacy. The HOA would assume the authority to add, modify and/or eliminate the rules and regulations used in the rental agreements and to determine HOA fees and the consequence for nonpayment.

In the interim, a Tiny Homes resident council has been charged with handling rules related to nuisance activities and securing training so residents will understand their rights, responsibilities and the legal issues inherent in overseeing an HOA. All of the Cass residential programs have resident councils and resident-elected officers. Moreover, two people utilizing Cass programs serve on the board of directors with full voice and vote. One individual is selected from the Activity Center for

Adults with Developmental Disabilities and the other lives in one of the Cass residential programs.

Currently, the residential representative on the board is Robert Prince. Robert was one of nine children. He was raised in the Brewster-Douglass Housing Projects by a single mother who worked a job and a half to provide for her family. As with many others in our country, he started abusing drugs in high school. When Robert arrived at Cass 40 years later, he walked with a limp, relied on a cane, had trouble hearing in one ear and wore glasses and casual, loose-fitting, donated clothing. Early on, his case manager asked him what he wanted to change about his life. Robert explained with both his voice and hand motions that he had three goals: to stop taking drugs; to find a job; and to move into an apartment. Eleven months later, after a few fits and starts with sobriety, he had achieved all three. More than that, he restored a relationship with his adult son. Robert talks with pride about buying his grandson diapers and wipes. He drives to visit his son's family in a used car that he purchased with the wages from his job. When the board considers the need for housing, drug rehabilitation, employment or healthcare, Robert has a unique and important perspective to bring to the discussions.

There is one more detail to mention. Cass will use the seven-year rental period to decide on the CC&Rs (covenants, conditions and restrictions) for the recorded deeds.

Above: The Corktown row house is sandwiched between a house slated for renovation and Most Holy Trinity Church. The exterior of the building is freshly painted since the structure was included in the 2017 Corktown Neighborhood Tour. The interior awaits rehab. Right: A group of volunteers from the University of Michigan used Michigan Central Station's 18-story tower as a backdrop. At that point in time, it didn't have windows and the mammoth building was secured only with a barbed-wire fence. (Urban explorers occasionally went inside to look around or add some signage. The words "Save the Depot" are exhibited on the top ledge in this photo.) Over 1,000 windows were installed in 2015. Other favorite places for photo shoots in Detroit include: the Heidelberg Project, the Motown Museum, the Packard Plant and Belle Isle (you can position the people on the tip of the island park so that both the U.S. and Canada are in the background).

Rolly ████ Just think of the $3 billion dollars we just gave away to Iran "our enemy" could have bought for our homeless people here. Just saying.
Like · Reply · September 14, 2016 at 9:30am

Doug ████ Yup. Then the city/county/state goes, yah baby... Tax revenue. Then they're homeless again and how much has been spent by who to get the same result?
Like · Reply · September 15, 2016 at 10:53am

Kass ████ Who is paying for the home, utilities. Property taxes, and upkeep? It's a good thought, I just don't see how those folks with no jobs in an area with little jobs can afford it.
Like · Reply · September 15, 2016 at 9:03pm

Glenn ████ Who's paying for these houses gee I wonder I'm gonna go with us tax payer's
Like · Reply · September 16, 2016 at 5:27pm

16

Funding and Costs

WHEN I HAD had enough of late payments and partial payments from my investment property, I decided it was time to sell the duplex. I never really wanted to fix someone else's toilet or garbage disposal, or to cut someone else's grass or shovel their snow ... I never got used to picking up used beer cups or condoms. I called Char Rosenbaum, a former Cass board member and real estate agent, and asked her if she would sell the property. She and her business partner, Christine Lapinski, walked through the brick building and inspected the backyard, which had an extra lot and one of the few inground pools in Detroit. (I was sick of cleaning the pool, too.)

Char and Christine weren't sure what price to put on the listing. They indicated they would check into comparables and get back with me. In the meantime, I notified the tenants that I was going to sell the duplex in the next couple of months and that I couldn't guarantee the new owner would want to keep them on as renters. One by one, they relocated. Only the "cat burier" remained.

He didn't start scouting for some place new to rent at all. Rather, he actively—and systematically—destroyed the apartment. Perhaps in a tribute to Tiger Stadium, he took a baseball bat to a large-screen TV and left all the pieces of shattered glass strewn across the living room floor. Then he used his Louisville slugger to break all the wooden spindles on the staircase. He lodged knives into the walls of a bedroom and spray painted anatomically correct impressions of naked women on the basement bricks. Did I mention that he unplugged the refrigerator, which was full of food? The kitchen smelled worse than an unattended dog kennel. What's more, even with 24 hours notice, he refused to let agents in for showings.

I was in Washington state (looking at Quixote Village) when Char called and said she thought we could get $210,000 for the duplex which made me buoyant because I had paid $158,000 for it 12 years ago in 2002. I only wished my parents had been alive. I could still hear my father telling me what a horrible investment it was to buy in Detroit. In fact, during the recession of 2008, I was underwater on the property and I wondered if I would ever break even.

Twenty-six interested buyers went through at least one of the apartments in five days. Corktown, just as much as Midtown, was seeing an incredible resurgence. Its proximity to downtown and new restaurants and stores made it a magnet for young professionals and families. Several of the offers exceeded the asking price. One bidder sent a handwritten testimonial letter explaining why his offer should be selected. I went with the highest bid. After a deduction linked to the home inspection, the duplex sold for a cool $270,000. When people ask me about what happens if a Tiny Home owner makes a profit selling their house, I think back to the day I learned that I would have an extra $112,000 to use for a retirement house and I answer in my head, *I hope so*. Of course, there are no tiny house comparables in Detroit today and no one can predict what the homes will be worth in the future. I am relatively confident that gentrification won't occur in the area of our campus anytime soon and, if some of the houses sell to people with a little more money to spend, some economic diversity is always desirable.

There are three questions asked by nearly everyone:

1. Where did the money come from to build the Cass Tiny Homes?
2. How much do the Tiny Homes cost?
3. How do the bills get paid once the homes are occupied?

Let me address this "holy trinity" of questions in order.

First and foremost, no government money was used in the project. We decided this early on because government grants can swell expenses and because federal, state and county/city awards can be reduced or eliminated at any time. The last thing you want to say to someone with housing insecurity is that he or she can become a homeowner in seven years and, then, mid-course, return to inform that person that the funds have been cut and so the deal is off.

Cass Tiny Homes employed what I call the "Stone Soup" development plan. You probably remember the tale about a stranger (or strangers, depending on the variation of the story you know) convincing people in a village that he could make soup out of water and a stone. The newcomer fills his pot at the river and adds a rock before placing it on an open fire. The villagers are curious about what he is doing and they listen to him describing the tasty soup he stirs. Occasionally, the man samples the broth and comments that it is delicious but that it would be better with a smidgen of this ingredient or that. Each time a villager volunteers the needed vegetable or seasoning, the stranger gratefully adds it to the cooking container. Finally, he removes the stone and all of the villagers enjoy the scrumptious soup. Some say the villagers were tricked into donating. I like to believe that the stranger taught them to be philanthropic. Once they surrendered what they had available, everyone enjoyed a hearty meal rather than leaving some with nothing or a flavorless, nutrition-negative cup of warm water.

Funding

When we started telling people about our unique housing project, all we had were photos from the Internet of tiny houses that existed elsewhere. I put them into a PowerPoint presentation to illustrate what we were going to build in Detroit. I talked about how it was going to be good, but we just needed a few ingredients. The truth is that without significant support, we couldn't have built anything. Our board of directors requested a business plan for the virgin program. It took approximately five months to complete the detailed document, but the storytelling started before the plan was complete.

The very first group to help make it into something real was the RNR Foundation. RNR board member Richard Lord and his wife, Sue Jeffers, introduced us to the family foundation. They had done fantastic work across the country with camps and schools. Moreover, RNR had already paid for college students to intern at Cass during the summers. The undergrads came north from Rollins College in Winter Park, Florida. I edited the PowerPoint presentation and submitted it with a grant request to RNR for pre-development dollars. They generously awarded Cass enough money to engage a grant writer, purchase architectural drawings and hire an owner's representative for six months.

Next, the Ford Fund expressed an interest. Ford had also been a longtime supporter in terms of corporate sponsorships and volunteer teams. Workers from Ford Motor Co. assisted in the Cass kitchen, helped harvest a plot of potatoes, and handled painting projects and demolition work. That was where I met Jim Vella, the President of the Ford Fund. He helped me throw a gigantic sofa out of the third-floor window of an apartment building we had to empty before renovations could begin. The Ford Fund committed $400,000 to the Tiny Homes and sent regular volunteers to assist with construction and landscaping.

I was then asked to do a short TEDx-style talk as part of the annual conference in East Lansing. This was a meeting of pastors and lay people from more than 800 United Methodist churches from both of Michigan's peninsulas. I pulled out my old "battery-less" laptop and PowerPoint once more and tried to make the script fit into their five-minute time allotment. I failed, running well beyond my presentation period, but it was a forgiving audience. Churches started asking if they could get involved. Farmington Hills Orchard, Birmingham First, Livonia Nardin Park—all United Methodist churches, along with St. Kenneth's Catholic Church in Livonia and Ann Arbor First Presbyterian were the first to shoulder some of the heavy lifting around fundraising.

The day that Orchard made their check presentation was unforgettable. The group was small—five or six people. It included the chairperson, 10th-grader Sarah Hume. She heard my spiel in their church fellowship hall and managed to get herself elected to chair the ad hoc committee. She handed me an envelope with a check for $22,000 and she said there would be more coming. Obviously, we posed together for iPhone pictures. Then, Pastor Amy Mayo-Moyle explained that the committee vice chairperson wasn't present because he couldn't skip his third-grade classes. Nine-year-old Alex Hamilton single-handedly raised $300 for the Tiny Homes.

We just kept stirring the proverbial pot. Three members of the Junior League of Detroit attended the press conference for the first home in September 2016. Carmella Leiter, Myra Rodriguez and Michelle Agosta were impressed with the idea and got us invited to make a speech at their meeting in Grosse Pointe. The Junior League of Detroit does amazing work. They rehabilitate and decorate a huge showhouse every other year and open it up to the community for tours. They use the proceeds from the event to provide financial support to organizations that work with women and children. You know what *I* did. I took the PowerPoint presentation (like Chris Garner with his bone scanner in *The Pursuit of Happyness*), and after I found the right building, I explained the Cass Tiny Homes program. The women's group voted to designate their Holiday Jubilee proceeds to Cass.

The McGregor Fund gave us a grant to pay our owner representative for another 18 months. Comerica Bank, through the Community Foundation for Southeast Michigan, provided funding to pay for the legal services required to obtain clear titles for the lots before we began building. The response to our needs was astounding! Our agency had never asked people to contribute at those levels before, and we were amazed at the charitable nature of the community. The development process dramatically changed our understanding of fundraising. People want to be involved in solving societal problems but someone must ask.

Construction Costs

Rich Scheck, our LEED-certified volunteer, said that construction would be about $161 per square foot. That meant that our homes would run between $48,000 and $62,000 depending on the size. Those amounts sounded extremely high to us until we conducted some research. When we compared the numbers from other tiny house developments, our estimates were in the middle. The least expensive were smaller—built by volunteers and without plumbing, electrical, heating or a kitchen. The most expensive houses cost over $100,000 per unit. The construction quality is superior. The sturdy structures are mostly built by professionals, and they include some plumbing and heating/cooling. Each of the more expensive villages contain very attractive community buildings, as well. There are variations of amenities. (See the comparison snapshot on pages 52-53.)

When we compared our financial projections with Habitat for Humanity numbers, our costs were between one-half and one-third of their houses. Then, we looked at construction expenses for subsidized housing. One Detroit nonprofit paid over $300,000 to rehab one-bedroom apartments for formerly homeless adults. They used low-income housing tax credits—which are popular—but they are the most expensive form of permanent housing. We also evaluated the cost of our homes weighed agasint other institutional settings such as hospitals, jails/prisons and nursing home units.

There aren't any living areas in the new Little Caesars Arena currently under construction in downtown Detroit, but the stadium will be the new *home* of both the Detroit Pistons (basketball) and the Detroit Red Wings (hockey). In May 2017, the

Type of Living Spaces	Approximate Unit Cost to Build	Source
A Basic Tent	$100	Local Retailer
Tiny House without Electric or Plumbing	$2,000-$4,000	Tiny House Villages
Cass Tiny Home	$45,000-$65,000	
Quixote Village House	$102,000	Ginger Segel, White Paper
Prison Cell	$94,000-$102,000	Connecticut General Assembly - #s from 1990s
Habitat House	$80,000-$155,000	Habitat for Humanity affiliate websites
Subsidized One-Bedroom Apartment	$150,000-300,000	HUD
Teaching Hospital Patient Room	$1,500,000	Quora

Michigan Strategic Fund approved additional taxpayer financing that will bring the total cost of the development up to $863 million—though slightly more than $324 million of that will be public money. Originally, the projection for stadium new construction was $450 million.

Our goal was to take advantage of the economies of scale (building multiple homes at a time), repurposing materials and/or utilizing new donated items, and making extensive use of volunteer teams to contain labor costs. We aimed at keeping the construction expenses on par with a luxury car: $40,000 to $50,000. The soft costs played havoc with our budget. Adding engineering drawings ran $2,500 per home. The foundations—excavating, constructing concrete footings, masonry wall flooring, backfilling, compacting the dirt and pouring the concrete slab required another $12,000-$15,000 per house. Then, the cost of running the utilities in from the street (saw cutting the existing pavement, tapping into the existing sanitary sewer and water main, excavating and installing new water and sanitary services and running new leads into the building for final connection) was a $6,800 expense. We fought constantly to control costs whenever possible.

There were two exceptions. We paid for spray foam insulation (which was three times more expensive than the fiberglass rolls of insulation). It was our contention that the investment was critical to reducing the loss of energy long-term. The insulation also acts as a sound barrier. The other place we spent extra money was on the vinyl siding. The idea was to make the exterior of the homes as maintenance-free as possible.

Some people questioned why our homes cost as much as they did. They reported seeing tiny houses that were considerably cheaper on Facebook or Pinterest. I would counter with several questions: Did those houses have heating/cooling systems? Was there insulation? How about water or electricity? All of these features impact costs (and for our residents, resale value). Then I asked if their equivalent was on a trailer.

Mobile tiny houses don't make a lot of sense for poor people. A fully loaded tiny home trailer weighs about 10,000 pounds. How are they going to pull it with a bicycle? Where are they going to park it long-term? There are a number of costs related to moving a tiny home: buying or renting a 4-by-4 truck and trailer, insurance and gasoline at 8 to 10 miles per gallon. There is also the maintenance of the vehicle and the trailer if you own them. Your tally for mobile freedom has to take land-use fees, mobile Internet, propane, etc. into account.

In order to compare apples to apples, there is a checklist of construction costs to consider for tiny homes:

- ☑ **Land Acquisition or Rental Fees.** Purchasing property needs to embrace title survey and insurance, closing costs, legal representation as well as the price of the land itself. Renting space requires legal counsel and insurance, too. You will also want to build moving expenses into a rental budget because the landlord may decide not to renew the lease.

- ☑ **Environmental Assessment and Possible Remediation.** The land and water quality must be tested. If issues are identified during the first phase, you will probably need to conduct another test or two. If there is contamination that exceeds your state standards, remediation will be required before construction can commence.

- ☑ **Demolition.** Buildings are expensive to raze and remove. The one dilapidated duplex on our 26 lots cost $13,000 for demolition and disposal. This is not a project for volunteer teams.

- ☑ **Architectural Plans.** Detroit didn't require us to submit plans signed by an architect but drawings were needed nonetheless. We were able to purchase most for between $300 and $1,500. FYI: Most plans are only good for one address. Frequently, they needed to be modified for regional weather conditions.

- ☑ **Engineering Drawings.** These are required when utilities must be brought into a new building. Ours ran $2,500 per home.

- ☑ **Construction Costs.** Construction costs are divided between materials and labor. Labor is by far the larger figure. Inspection fees should be incorporated into this amount. City inspections are mandated throughout the process and before a municipality will issue a Certificate of Occupancy.

- ☑ **Grading and Concrete Replacement.** At the end of the construction phase, the surface must be sloped or graded to allow for runoff drainage. This often requires heavy machinery. Likewise, once the contractors are finished, sidewalks which were removed to bring the utility lines into a house must be replaced.

- ☑ **Insurance.** The owner must secure builder's risk insurance for the project. Applying for this special policy mandates that you produce a copy of the general contractor's worker's comp, vehicle insurance, as well as the executed contract. Our agency had to be named as an "additional insured" on the general contractor's liability as well. Finally, we had to describe the role that volunteers would play during the construction project for the insurance company.

- ☑ **Staff.** Someone needs to have the responsibility of overseeing the project and, if you are utilizing volunteers, someone should supervise their activities.

Security personnel are needed to watch the construction site. Having a grant writer or fund raiser is beneficial.

☑ **Landscaping and Fencing.** The contractors kill anything green, which means everything turns to mud when it rains. We used Grade B sod for the front yards (the B designation means it has some weeds). We seeded the backyards. Volunteers managed all of the flowerbeds and trees. Nancy McNab, president of Sun & Shade Designs, handled the first house alone even though her truck full of plants broke down the day before the press conference. Leonard "Zack" DiGrande of American Fence & Supply Company obtained fencing previously used at area school ballfields. He cut it down to size for us and volunteer teams were able to install the repurposed chain-link boundary maker.

☑ **Appliances and Furniture.** Stoves, refrigerators, microwaves, washers, dryers, etc. may or may not be included in the construction costs. Tenants may want to bring a favorite piece of furniture or two but most sofas and chairs will not fit into the compact living areas of a Tiny Home. Some of the furniture we used was donated but most was purchased.

☑ **Odds and Ends.** Mailboxes, address plaques, towel bars, toilet paper holders, shower rods and curtains, shower mats, waste cans, pots, pans, towels, art, shelving and other items may or may not be included in construction budget.

Annual Operational Costs

Of course, when considering how much tiny houses cost you need to be mindful of operational charges, too. What is the price tag for people to live in the houses, and who will pay the bills? Ongoing operational expenses include utilities, taxes, insurance, maintenance and repairs. If there are services attached to the housing, the costs will have to include staff expenses and program supplies.

Most tiny house villages rely on the monthly "rent" money to offset expenses. These monthly amounts range from $30 at Opportunity Village to a maximum of $380 at Community First! Village. Many organizations also expect residents to contribute volunteer hours to either reduce expenses or raise funds using micro-enterprises such as the Dignity Dogs food carts at Dignity Village and the Occupy Madison Village store (wood products).

In the case of HUD-funded programs (like Quixote Village and Hickory Crossing), government grants pay for all or part of the fair market rent amount. A resident contributes one-third of his or her income (if the person has an income) and a voucher pays the difference. So, if the fair market rent is $600 but one-third of the resident's income is $200, a government subsidy will pay the outstanding $400 a month. Vouchers can be either portable, meaning it stays with the resident, or stationary, meaning it remains with the project/building. Either way, with subsidized housing, government assistance is demanded indefinitely. Obviously, tax dollars are used with other types of housing. Jail and prison cells call for government funds. It costs $38,809 to keep an inmate in a prison cell for one year in Michigan according to the Vera Institute of Justice's 2015 figures. Medicaid pays $47,000 annually for a nursing bed.

It is not true for Habitat for Humanity homes. The residents assume mortgages from the nonprofit for a period of between seven and 30 years. Prospective homeowners put in "sweat equity" and then assume the recurring bills. There is no subsidy involved. Habitat for Humanity uses a no-interest mortgage.

Although Habitat has an excellent asset-building strategy, people coming out of homelessness and others living on minimum wages/part-time wages cannot qualify for a mortgage even if they have saved up enough money for a down payment and closing costs. It was for that reason we designed a different homeownership program. There was some hesitation about using the "rent to own" terminology because it generally designates a business that practices predatory lending. (Some payday loans charge 400 percent interest.) We coined the phrase "rent then own" as it more accurately captures our program. The residents do not pay for the homes. Instead, their rent money is used to pay for most of the operational expenses.

Rent for the Cass Tiny Homes is calculated by square footage. A 250-square-foot home costs $250 monthly. A 300-square-foot one requires a $300 payment. It follows then that 350- and 400-square-foot houses have $350 and $400 rental fees respectfully. Originally we planned to build 300- to 400-square-foot homes, but then we dropped down to include 250-square-foot homes to accommodate people whose income comes from Social Security Disability. (They receive roughly $750 monthly or about $9,000 annually and, thus, the smaller homes wouldn't consume more than one-third of a person's earnings.) For the metropolitan Detroit rental market, these are very affordable rates. According to HUD, the 2016 Fair Market Rents for an efficiency apartment is $532 and a one-bedroom apartment is $658.[44] Therefore, the Tiny Homes renters are paying roughly half of what they would shell out elsewhere for comparable-sized housing without the option of home ownership.

Since the money to build the houses was raised prior to the homes being occupied, you may be wondering why Cass is charging any rent at all. Why don't we simply give the properties to the residents right away? The seven-year period was planned to insure that once the renters became homeowners they won't lose their homes due to financial vulnerability. Other than foreclosure, homeowners forfeit their houses in Michigan for two reasons: failure to pay property taxes; and/or being in arrears with their water bills. Thus, Cass pays for four basic bills using the rent income: property taxes, water bills, insurance premiums and the bill for security system monitoring during the seven rental years. This extended phase will help people develop a pattern of bill paying and saving for emergencies so that they will be positioned to keep the homes after they become owners. Once the houses belong to them, they stop paying Cass rent and assume the four bills the agency had been handling on their behalf.

The Tiny Home Business Plan projected income and expenses for a period of 10 years. It anticipated some building/property expenses. Cass also established a contingency fund ($5,000 per house/or $125,000 total) and deposited it in an interest-generating account to cover the repair and replacement of appliances, plumbing, roofs, etc. We have the goal of starting a separate endowment account, as well, to respond to needs identified by the home owners organization in the future.

Above: FOX 2's Amy Andrews interviewed 9-year-old Alex Hamilton and 17-year-old Sarah Hume of Farmington Hills and their pastor, Amy Mayo-Moyle. Orchard United Methodist Church raised $40,000 to sponsor the Victorian tiny home. Right: Best-selling author and philanthropist Mitch Albom presents a $25,000 check from his S.A.Y. Detroit foundation to our owner's representative, Stacy Conwell-Leigh, for the Tiny Homes. Photo by Jordan Ozimek. Permission granted by SAY Detroit.

Roxann ███████ How can we help
Like · Reply · September 14, 2016 at 2:04pm

LaTasha ███████ How freaking AWESOME.... how can we help?????
Like · Reply · September 14, 2016 at 11:47pm

Antony ███████ How can i be a part if this?
Like · Reply · September 17, 2016 at 5:23am

17

Donated Materials

THE FORMER OWNERS of the ranch house I bought on Lake Huron were kind enough to leave a few bookshelves, a king-size bed and some outdoor furniture. It was a good thing because the purchase didn't leave me with any extra cash. Ed Hingelberg, who has worked at Cass almost as long as I have, parted with his mother's La-Z-Boy rocking chairs and a couch for the house. I had been quite fond of his mother, Marie, so the furnishings meant a lot.

My mother would have been flabbergasted that I accepted the items. I had never appreciated "used" stuff growing up. In fact, I was mortified when she would stop the car on trash day and make me hop out to grab whatever it was that she saw on the curb. What would people think about me picking through garbage to snatch an old lamp, an ironing board, someone's high chair or a mat? I'd climb back into the station wagon totally humiliated and my mother would be on cloud nine, talking about what she would do with her find. Maybe it stemmed from the fact that, more often than not, I wore somebody else's "hand-me-down" clothes growing up. They were perfectly fine and they almost fit—but I always wanted something new.

The other thing that would mystify my mother is that one of the bonuses of my lake house in Applegate is its rummage sale location. The ranch is right in the middle of the annual yard sale that snakes along M-25 for 150 miles by the shores of Lake Huron. People sell and shop for three straight days in August, from south of Port Huron all the way up to the tip of the thumb near Port Austin and down again to Sebewaing, Michigan on Saginaw Bay. It's something to behold. "You got any boat motors?" a bargain veteran yells through his open passenger-side window, idling just long enough to hear an answer. The first vehicles belong to the professionals. The pros are looking for under priced antiques, rare coins and tools. They are akin to heat-seeking rockets. Next, families in minivans, full-size vans and some pickup trucks stop and shop. They want children's clothing, books, games, DVDs and recreational equipment. Then, there are the folks who are out for a leisurely drive. They like to chat but rarely do they part with their money.

My cousins Robin, Raymond and Linda come up for the rummage sale weekend to sell their used merchandise and we have a blast even though the village population is less than the census of Cass' residential programs. When there is a break in the customer traffic, you can hear the waves of the lake. In the evening, after the shoppers are gone, you stand transfixed under the uninterrupted sky. It is awash with the light of hundreds of stars both living and dead. The house doesn't have Internet connection, cable television or cellphone accessibility. Everyone is forced to unplug which, as my smartphone reminds me, is demanded periodically. Most afternoons, the fresh air and the quiet lulls me to sleep in Ed's mother's comfortable chair for a nap that magically obliterates stress.

Recycling is a way of life at Cass. Since 2007, salvaging trash has created jobs for the unemployed adults, and in 2016, we discovered that reclaiming materials could be equally effective for building construction. One of our board members Bonnie Mellos hosted what we refer to as a "parlor meeting" at her home in Grosse Pointe. In short, she invited about 20 couples over for refreshments and I was given the opportunity to explain the Tiny Homes project to raise both awareness and funds. It went smoothly. People asked educated questions about the math, construction procedures and the application process. Then, one woman said that she was renovating her kitchen. Could Cass use her old granite countertops in a tiny home?

After I picked myself up off of Bonnie's hardwood floor, I said something like, "Hell, *I* don't have granite counter tops." Then, remembering that I am a clergy person, I continued, "Of course, we would be happy to pick them up and give you donation documentation so you can have a tax write-off."

Our obsession became building with the best quality materials, donated whenever possible, for the least amount of money. One contractor gave us cultured stone for the Tudor chimney—he had extra at the end of a commercial job. Another man provided all the roofing materials for the same house. People gave us pavers and bricks and backsplash tile. They dropped off interior doors and lighting.

New materials were donated, too. Cora Glass, one of our former interns and now a deacon at Garrett-Evangelical Theological Seminary persuaded her cousin Jon Saul to donate one bundle of two-by-fours, one bundle of two-by-sixes and a bundle of plywood. He got his employer, American Manufacturing, to give us a bundle and Midwest Timber to donate two more! Since we didn't have a truck with the capacity to haul all of the wood, Jon even convinced his trucker buddy to deliver it all for free!

HermanMiller helped furnish the homes with $6,000-worth of excellently crafted folding tables, three styles of chairs and Hang-It-Alls (which have 14 hangers with colorful balls that are strong enough to hold overcoats, bath towels and bags). Home Depot provided $25,000-worth of building materials and sent work crews to the construction site to set them up.

Women from the Ann Arbor United Church of Christ made curtains and bought blinds. Rick Pethoud, married to our volunteer coordinator, Sue Pethoud, built a ladder and railings for one of the homes with a loft. The Junior League of Detroit supplied housewarming kits with towels and kitchen supplies. The youth of Chelsea gave and planted the flowers at two Tiny Homes as did the Junior League of Detroit. The Huntington Woods Seed & Sod Garden Club paid for two grown trees, including their installation. The Erb Family Foundation provided additional trees, a tree plan for community and rain barrels for harvesting water.

It was like an urban barn-raising marathon where people just showed up, ready to help—only they came with loads of the materials needed to erect the buildings.

HermanMiller donated attractive and functional folding chairs and tables for the homes.

Above: Ann Baxter, a member of the Junior League of Detroit, made the three leaded and beveled glass windows that accent the front of the house they sponsored. Below: Rick Pethoud did the woodwork to create gorgeous stairs and railings for one of the loft areas.

Patricia ███████ This is awesome news!
Like · Reply · September 17, 2016 at 10:16pm
Phyllis ███████ David Wolfe you are marvelous! What a beautiful brain
you have BRAVO! 💜
Like · Reply · September 14, 2016 at 11:47pm

18

Going Viral Once More

Cass Tiny Homes Media Stories

"Building up tiny houses to break down asset inequality." *Stateside*. Cynthia Canty. Michigan Public Radio. May 31, 2016.

"Tiny homes project aims to stabilize neighborhood, house Detroit homeless." Ian Thibodeau. MLive. May 18, 2016.

"A Community of Tiny Homes Could Help Detroit's Homeless." Robin Runyan. Curbed Detroit. May 19, 2016.

"Help Build Tiny Homes For Homeless Detroiters." Ardelia Lee. Daily Detroit. WJBK. May 19, 2016.

"Group using tiny houses to help Detroit homeless problem." *Detroit Today*. Hannah Saunders. WDET. May 19, 2016.

"What Tiny Houses Could Mean for The Poor in Detroit" Stephen Henderson. WDET. May 19, 2016.

"A low-income, tiny house community is coming to Detroit." Paulette Parker. Michigan Public Radio. May 20, 2016.

"'Tiny Homes' leaves a huge impact." Selena Aguilera. *Metro Times*. May 25, 2016.

"Tiny homes for the homeless." Corrie Goldberg. WDIV. May 29, 2016.

"Big dreams, tiny houses: Detroit project offers affordable, rent-to-own housing." Maureen Feighan. *The Detroit News*. May 31, 2016.

"Building up tiny houses to break down asset inequality." Lindsey Scullen. Interlochen Public Radio. May 31, 2016.

"Dream, tiny houses." MI area UMC reporter. June 1, 2016.

"Tiny houses are trendy, minimalist and often illegal." *NewsHour*. Rebecca Beitsch. PBS. July 6, 2016.

Lite Breakfast Show. Sonuljit Singh. Kuala Lumpur, Malaysia Radio Broadcast. July 8, 2016.

"Tiny house trend grows as people focus on essentials." Maureen Feighan. *The Detroit News*. July 8, 2016.

"Cass Community Social Services is building a tiny house village for the homeless in Detroit." Gretchen Gates. TinyHomeTour.com. July 22, 2016.

"25 tiny houses being built for low-income Detroit residents." Associated Press. ABC. July 10, 2016.

"Lessons to be had from tiny homes" Floyd Perras. *Winnipeg Sun*. July 13, 2016.

"Cass Community Services: Building a Ladder." InterFaith Leadership Council of Metropolitan Detroit. July 19, 2016.

"Street Beat: Helping The Homeless." Associated Press. CBS Detroit. August 10, 2016.

"25 tiny houses being built for low-income Detroit residents." Associated Press. *The Monroe News*. August 10, 2016.

"Places to Stay: Communities for All People in Need." TinyHouseCommunity.com. August 11, 2016.

"Detroit nonprofit creating tiny houses community." Chris Ehrmann. *Crain's Detroit Business*. August 12, 2016.

"Cass Group Will Build 25 Tiny Homes for Low-Income Detroiters." Annabel Ames. Deadline Detroit. September 8, 2016.

"Tiny houses in Detroit aim to improve lives of poor, community." Matt Helms. *Detroit Free Press*. September 8, 2016.

"Detroit tiny house project is 'game changer.'" Maureen Feighan. *The Detroit News*. September 8, 2016.

"Tiny house model home tour in Detroit" (photo gallery). Bryan Mitchell. *The Detroit News*. September 8, 2016.

"Look Inside The Delightful Tiny House That Could Be A "Game Changer" For Detroit." Shianne Nocerini. Daily Detroit. September 8, 2016.

"Tiny houses in Detroit aim to improve lives of poor, community." Matt Helms. *Lansing State Journal*. September 8, 2016.

"Cass Community Social Services and Ford Host Tiny Home Open House." Roz Edward. Michigan Chronicle. September 8, 2016.

"Ford to help fund construction of $1.5 million tiny home neighborhood in Detroit." Dana Afana. MLive. September 8, 2016.

"Cass Community Social Services tiny home community: Renderings." Tanya Moutzalias. MLive. September 8, 2016.

"New project in west Detroit could help tackle homelessness, poverty" Pryia Mann. ClickOnDetroit. com. September 8, 2016.

"Detroit tiny house project is 'game changer.'" Associated Press. WDIV. September 8, 2016.

"Group using tiny houses to help Detroit homeless problem." Associated Press. WJBK. September 8, 2016.

"Tiny homes popping up on Detroit vacant lots." Associated Press. WXYZ. September 8, 2016.

"This tiny house could be a game changer for the low-income population in Detroit." Robin Runyan. Curbed Detroit. September 8, 2016.

"A Community of Tiny Homes Could Help Detroit's Homeless." (repost of Curbed Detroit article by Robin Runyan). Current Affairs. September 8, 2016.

"Nonprofit Unveils First of 25 Tiny Homes in Detroit." Allan Lengal. Deadline Detroit. September 8, 2016.

"A Community of Tiny Homes Could Help Detroit's Homeless." demmiblue's Journal (info off Curbed). DemocraticUnderground.com. September 9, 2016.

"This Tiny House Community Will Turn Homeless People Into Homeowners." Kate Abbey-Lambertz. Huffington Post. September 9, 2016.

"A Community of Tiny Homes Could Help Detroit's Homeless." (info off Curbed). MSN. September 9, 2016.

"Tiny homes aim to help poor become homeowners in Detroit." Matt Helms. *USA Today*. September 9, 2016.

"A Community of Tiny Homes Could Help Detroit's Homeless." Cat. Dark Light Daily. September 10, 2016.

"Detroit organization unveils first home in $1.5M tiny house community." Kim Slowey. Construction Dive. September 12, 2016.

"A Community of Tiny Homes Could Help Detroit's Homeless." (info. off Curbed). Tiny House Town. September 13, 2016.

"This Tiny House Project Will Turn Homeless People Into Homeowners." David Wolfe. Facebook. (12m Views, 77k Likes, 210k Shares). September 13, 2016.

"Problem Solving Must-Reads: Tiny Homes For The Homeless." Gillian McGoldrick. *The Philadelphis Citizen*. September 14, 2016.

"Welcome to Micro Week, which starts right now." Robin Runyan. Curbed Detroit. September 19, 2016.

"Tiny Homes May Hold Key to Breaking Poverty Cycle." Wendy Joan Biddlecombe. HopefulHeadlines.org. September 20, 2016.

"Ford Contributes $400k to Innovative tiny Homes Project in Detroit." The News Wheel. September 20, 2016.

"What will the next round of tiny homes in Detroit look like?" Robin Runyan. Curbed Detroit. September 21, 2016.

"Ford Motor Company Fund playing major role in Detroit transformation, invested $20 million last year." Marge Sorge. DetroitUnspun. October 6, 2016.

"City envy: we want tiny houses for the homeless like Detroit." Flo Wales Bonner. Time Out London. October 9, 2016.

"Ford Fund invests $5 million in Detroit Neighborhood."
AJ Williams. Michigan Chronicle. October 13, 2016.

Mandy ▓▓▓▓ This would be great if it were true. I live in Michigan, not far from Detroit, and have heard absolutely nothing about this on any kind of news source.
Like · Reply · October 15, 2016 at 11:58am

"Tiny Living For The Not-so-small Life." Lori Bitter. MediaPost. October 17, 2016.

"Detroit is getting a neighborhood of tiny homes that homeless people rent to own." Dana Varinsky. Business Insider. October 18, 2016.

"Detroit is getting a neighborhood of tiny homes that homeless people rent to own." Dana Varinsky. SQ FTGate (repost of Business Insider story). October 18, 2016.

"First Detroit Tiny House Village Lets Tenants Rent to Own." McKinley Corbley. Good News Network. October 20, 2016.

"Homeless People Can Rent To Own A Tiny House In Detroit." Frank Williams Jr. WYCD 99.5. October 20, 2016.

"Tiny Town: Detroit agency aims to bring city's homeless out of the cold." Weston Williams. The Christian Science Monitor. October 20, 2016.

CW50 - 10-21-16, Street Beat, "Street Beat: Helping The Homeless." *Street Beat*. CW50. October 21, 2016.

"This Community Is Fighting Homelessness With Homes—& We Need More of This." Tanvier Peart. The Stir. October 21, 2016.

"Private Charity Is Building An Entire Neighborhood of Tiny Homes For the Homeless to Rent to Own." Jack Burns. TheFreeThoughtProject.com. October 22, 2016.

"A tiny house village with the backing to succeed." Estee. Tiny House For Us. October 22, 2016.

Alisha ▓▓▓▓ If your reading this your parents will die within 5 years to break the curse you must copy this to 5 pictures good luck. If you love your mom post this to 20 picture. One girl ignored this and her mom died 365 days later. Sorry I can't ignore this because I love my mom.
Like · Reply · October 24, 2016 at 12:48pm

"Group Builds Tiny Homes For Low-Income Residents." Michaela Perira. HLN. October 28, 2016.

"A Detroit pastor and her church are building something big with tiny homes." Patricia Montemurri. Duke Divinity School Faith & Leadership. November 15, 2016.

"Tiny houses at a big crossroad." Catherine Kavanaugh. *Plastics News*. December 6, 2016.

"Tiny Houses in 2016: more tricked-out and eco-friendly - #6 An adorable tiny home for Detroit's low-income population." Jenny Xie. Curbed (national site). December 27, 2016.

"Detroit's biggest development news of 2016." Robin Runyan. Curbed Detroit. December 28, 2016.

"Detroit Is Introducing Tiny Homes For The Low-Income Population." *Professional Builder*. December 28, 2016.

"Tiny houses in Detroit." Buffalo Rising. December 30, 2016.

"Tiny House Movement: Helping the Homeless." Tiny House Blog. January 7, 2017.

"Tiny Homes For the Homeless." *Time to Build*. Joyanna Laughlin. Houseplans.com. January 17, 2017.

Everybody used to dream about being on "The Oprah Winfrey Show." Her endorsement could propel a person, a product, a book or an organization into the stratosphere. Cass was on "Oprah" but almost nobody knew it. Anderson Cooper came to Detroit to shoot a story about poverty. It included a stop at Mom's Place, our transitional housing program for homeless women and children. He interviewed one of the mothers who had spent some time living in her minivan with her three children before she entered Mom's Place. One day, her husband of 16 years left her. They divorced. She lost her job, and then the house. They ended up on Belle Isle, an island park in the middle of the Detroit River. When the mom, her two teenage sons and young daughter finally came in to Cass, we were able to help. In fact, by the time Anderson arrived, the family had moved on to permanent housing.

Practically no one contacted us after the program aired. Absolutely no one emailed, standard mailed or voice mailed. Why? Because the television show only referred to the program name, Mom's Place, rather than talking about the agency's name, Cass Community Social Services, which ran Mom's Place. It is more than disappointing to have had the national spotlight and still be unrecognized.

The story of Cass Tiny Homes on social media was something else altogether. As mentioned in the Introduction, David Wolfe's post garnered 13 million views in 10 months. As you have read, it seemed like everyone saw the video and thousands of people posted comments. Our telephones rang incessantly and more emails arrived around-the-clock. It grew frustrating because so many of the responses summed up the program as "giving homeless people free houses." The good news is that the experience prepared us for the NowThis Future video reactions. Using an unfortunately lit Skype interview, the video went up on June 15 and, in a month's time, had been viewed 30 million times.

The NowThis video was mostly correct. It was only misleading when it stated that residents were required to take mental health counseling and food preparation classes. Not everyone who is poor or formerly homeless is mentally ill. Mental health services are available at Cass but only some people need them and participating in them is always voluntary. In terms of cooking classes, who said low-income people don't know how to cook? Cass offers both food assistance and community meals for people who run out of food and/or for individuals who want to eat with others sometimes. These supports are optional, too. It is a rare exception when someone needs to be taught to cook. The video made it seem otherwise.

Our experience with the David Wolfe post had prepared us to cut and paste answers for Facebook messages and email inquiries. We warned those answering the switchboard about the expected onslaught and we told the executive staff how to handle incoming Internet requests. Scores of interested people e-mail blasted everyone listed on our web site directory. What we weren't prepared for was the volume of foreign inquires or sales. People from Australia, Japan, Italy, the U.K., Canada, Haiti, Kenya and Guyana asked for information and how to buy books. We really hadn't had much experience with international shipping and, so, it took us a week or two to figure out how to handle different currencies and to obtain the cheapest postage rates.

Once we understood international currency and postage, Curbed Detroit uploaded a video about our tiny homes project. It went viral, as well. Between NowThis and Curbed Detroit, the story had been viewed more than 75 million times in less than six months. I began to worry about what all this attention would mean to our residents. I remember reading that the people at Occupy Madison would no longer agree to be interviewed, citing "media fatigue." Would our people feel exploited? Would they think that being the subject of a story or 10 should entitle them to special "star" treatment? How would they react to the negative comments that appear with each and every online post? I have been disappointed by the venom and volume of online attacks concerning people who have been homeless and people who are low-income and people who live in Detroit and about ... How would they react if the comments were maliciously aimed at them? They didn't sign up for that. They don't deserve it either.

Above: A press conference held in September 2016 when media were invited to tour the first Cass Tiny Home on Elmhurst. Photo by Spencer Hayes. Permission granted by C & B Scene. Below: Screenshot of the story from Japan. Right: NowThis Future video that went viral in 2017.

「ホームレスの社会復帰」を徹底的にサポートする家

ホームレスの人たちへの支援と聞いたら、物資や食料の配給などを思い浮かべる。つまり、一時的には役立つのだけれど、すぐに消えてなくなってしまうものだ。だからこそ私は、アメリカの非営利団体「Cass Community Social...

TABI-LABO.COM

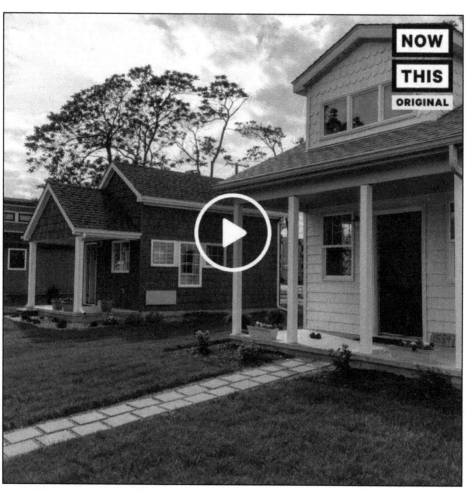

NOW
THIS
ORIGINAL

33,378,617 views

Bernadette ████ Brilliant idea, it should be copied here in Ireland. 😊 I love it.
Like · Reply · September 17, 2016 at 10:16pm

Mybaby ████ Need something like this in new Zealand
Like · Reply · September 14, 2016 at 4:28am

Rennie ████ Now why can't we do this. Great idea.
Like · Reply · February 12, 2017 at 6:22pm

MaryAnn ████ This is something that is needed in Branson, MO as well. I say this because there are people living in motel rooms and raising families in them as well. They pay anywhere from $125 to $155 per week for a motel room, where there are no kitchens to cook in. They can cook using electric skillets, crock pot, slow cookers. The city considers them homeless even though they have an address and get mail there. There are about 25 motels in the city that have individuals and children living in them.
Like · Reply · September 14, 2016 at 12:06am

Joanne ████ What a shame Australia doesn't do this
Like · Reply · September 14, 2016 at 4:48am

Adrian ████ I wished we have it here in U.K.
Like · Reply · September 14, 2016 at 6:23am

Kathy ████ Isn't this a terrific idea? Tucson, are you listening?
Like · Reply · September 14, 2016 at 8:14am

Penny ████ Need this in West Lafayette Indiana
Like · Reply · September 14, 2016 at 9:54am

Kathryn ████ They need to do something like this in Dayton, Ohio.
Like · Reply · September 14, 2016 at 12:11pm

Ashley ████ Wish they'd do that in small towns too. I know lots of people that live on couches and in cars that would really appreciate this.
Like · Reply · September 14, 2016 at 1:50pm

Janice ████ We need these in south Orange County California
Like · Reply · September 14, 2016 at 7:21pm

Rosaura ████ Would love to see this in Brazil.. Tiny houses for homeless and low income people, Gostaria de ver algo semelhante no Brasil.. mini casas para pessoas sem teto e de baixa renda.
Like · Reply · September 17, 2016 at 10:16pm

Marlon ████ the same should be done all over the world!!!!!
Like · Reply · September 15, 2016 at 1:21am

Joy ████ I would love to bring this to San Francisco. The city that has come up with this solution for homelessness: when the only shelter left for the poor is under a tree: cut the down the trees.
Like · Reply · September 17, 2016 at 10:16pm

Kathleen ████ This should be Across the country!!..oh and I Want one 👍👍
Like · Reply · December 26, 2016 at 8:30pm

19

Replication

WHEN I WAS a kid (and occasionally now when there's a heat wave), and someone opened up a fire hydrant, the cold water gushed out with tremendous force, and we would run through the thousands of gallons of water as if it were a sprinkler. Today when someone says it's like "drinking out of a fire hose," I usually envision the water from the hydrants shooting out with the force of Niagara Falls. The phrase is used to imply a near impossible task. As I mentioned in the last chapter, we learned how to respond to the volume of inquiries thanks to David Wolfe's post, but the NowThis Future video seemed to stimulate more difficult comments and requests.

One woman, who claimed to have eight years experience in the Tiny House movement, wrote to criticize everything about our model house—the design, the materials, the costs. She was certain that we had violated building codes. She urged us to hire a tiny house builder with experience.

Then, the writer indicated that I should review her credentials on LinkedIn. Her correspondence ended with these words: "It is imperative you do this right. Affordable housing for thousands, perhaps hundreds of thousands rests on your success or failure."

Most of the communication didn't make us feel like we were being squeezed in the jaws of a vise. Many people just had questions about the development. Here is one of my favorite email chains.

From: Tyler

To: Faith

Sent: June 29, 2017, 8:46 a.m

Subject: Tiny house book

I don't understand why you are selling your book. If you are so passionate about the project, why aren't you giving it away for free online as a PDF?

Sent: June 29, 2017, 9:57 a.m.

Faith wrote:

Tyler, We are selling the books because the sales will help fund additional houses. For $20, the buyer gets all the details that took us a year and a half to obtain and we use the proceeds to help build more homes in Detroit.

Sent: June 29, 2017, 11:08 a.m.

Tyler wrote:

So you think that the $20 from the book that you get is going to help more to help people with low in-comes find stable housing, than would spreading it freely to everyone all over the world? You are missing the forest for the trees.

Sent: June 29, 2017, 3:58 p.m.

Faith wrote:

Tyler, I'm so sorry, I'm afraid you are misunder-standing the focus of the book. The book is not meant for homeless/low-income people to use as a builder's guide or a map to find places that offer affordable tiny housing—if it were, then we would certainly consider offering it as a free guide.

I stopped answering his emails. I decided that if he couldn't afford $20 for a book, he probably wasn't ready to build a tiny house. It costs roughly that to buy a Monopoly game with the little green tiny house in the box. (After a little detective work, I learned that he works for a real estate agency that sells $600,000 homes in Texas.)

Then, there were a couple of hundred telephone calls. Most of them came from individuals who were thinking about doing something in their location. A few callers represented government agencies, but the bulk were from people representing nonprofit groups.

The conversations generally went like this:

> Caller: I didn't think I'd get you on the phone.
>
> Me: I'm sorry. Would you like my voicemail?
>
> Caller: No, no. I like what you are doing and I want to do the same thing in (name a location). Actually, I had the same idea (blank) years ago.
>
> Me: Good. How can I help you?
>
> Caller: Well, I have a some questions.
>
> Me: OK. Fire away.
>
> Caller: I don't know where to start. … (Long pause followed by unorganized and rapid filler for five or 10 minutes).
>
> Me: Do you have any land?
>
> Caller: No.

So I developed a list of questions to help folks figure out what they don't know and need to decide.

The more questions that can be answered, the closer an organization will be to creating a business plan for a tiny house village or tiny homes in a neighborhood. Imitation, as the adage goes, is the highest form of flattery.

Questions

1. Who will live in the house(s)?

2. Will it be a homogeneous population or a mixed group of people?

3. Can you list the qualifications they will need to be considered?

4. How and by whom will screening be conducted?

5. Will your tiny house(s) be on trailers or on foundations?

6. If trailers, where will the house(s) be built?

7. If trailers, where will the finished house(s) be parked?

8. If foundations, what type - basement, crawlspace, pier and beam or slab?

9. How is the identified property zoned - homeless shelter, campground, transitional or permanent encampment, residential or multi-family residential? Will you need a variance to place a tiny home on the property?

10. Are there minimal building requirements that limit the size of your house(s)?

11. What size(s) will you build?

12. Do you need to do environmental testing to ensure that the land and water is safe? Is the air quality a concern?

13. If so, have you identified a company that is qualified to conduct a Phase I environmental assessment?

14. Have you checked with your municipal departments to see what architectural drawings are required and whether they need to be signed and/or sealed?

15. Will you obtain the plans off the Internet or from a local professional and / or a school?

16. Will you build the house(s), or will you use a professional contractor, volunteers or a combination of all of these?

17. Do you have someone with the time and experience to serve as an owner's representative?

18. Have you secured insurance for the build?

19. Will you use new materials, repurposed materials or both?

20. Do you have someone who can comparison shop for the project so you get the best quality for the best prices?

21. How will you arrange the house(s)? Will they go on existing lots, use a village or a pocket neighborhood configuration?

22. If you decide to do a village setup, what will go in the houses and what communal buildings will be offered?

23. Have you developed a communication plan for your audiences, especially the neighborhood? Listening to area concerns and informing the community about your plans is key to minimizing NIMBY issues.

24. How will you pay for the construction—government grants, corporate donations, contributions from religious or other groups, individuals, a loan or a combination of these?

25. Will the residents rent, buy or both?

26. How much will residents pay?

27. Will the money from the residents cover the cost of operations once the house(s) are occupied or will you need to augment their money?

28. Is there a need for a governance structure? If yes, how will it function?

29. Will the program require or be strengthened by collaborators to build, operate and/or provide services for the development?

30. How much are you willing to pay for green building features and do you know what the return on the investment will be?

The need for affordable housing *and* home ownership is vast and global. The National Low Income Housing Coalition publishes an annual report that explores the gap between the nation's lowest income households and the availability of affordable housing. Their latest publication states that there is a shortage of 7.4 million affordable rental properties for extremely low income (ELI) households. Put another way, there are only 35 affordable homes available for every 100 ELI households and, the document asserts, there is "a shortage in every state and major metropolitan area.[45] Of course, every month of renting means that the extremely low income people aren't earning equity nor are they are they receiving mortgage interest tax deductions.

Internationally, I'll let one of the many e-mails I received tell the story.

Name: Adolfo

Email: txxxxx@gmail.com

Comment: Dear friend, My name is Adolfo. I am currently the Deputy Manager of Promotion and Development of the Municipality of Comas in Lima, Peru. I have under my responsibility the needs of 600 thousand people, of whom more than 250 thousand live in conditions of poverty. We are implementing housing security and agricultural development programs. I need to build 40,000 houses. Your initiative is the one we need. Please, I would like to implement your homes in the city of Lima in Peru. We would save tens of thousands of lives. A hug,

Adolfo

Cass staff member Geneal Martin was captured cooling off with a volunteer team member from Portland, Oregon. We didn't remove the cap. We understood that doing so would have reduced water pressure and could have impaired firefighters' efforts to extinguish a fire. But since it was shooting out like a water cannon, we couldn't resist having a little fun.

Tiny House Villages being Planned, in Progress or Recently Completed

A Tiny Home for Good – Syracuse, New York
Five 300-sq ft tiny houses built on vacant lots by A Tiny Home for Good
Ballard – Seattle, Washington
Five 96-sq. ft. by Nickelsville on City of Seattle Property
Emerald Village – Eugene, Oregon
Twenty-Two 150-288-sq ft by Square One on Square One Property
Georgetown Village – Seattle, Washington
Twelve 96 sq ft transitional housing by Nickelsville on City of Seattle Property
Infinity Village – Nashville, Tennessee
Six 60-sq ft residences by Infinity Fellowship on Green Street Church of Christ Property
My Tiny House Project – Los Angeles, California
Forty 50-sq ft by Starting Human on Starting Human Property
Othello Village – Seattle, Washington
Sixty 96 sq ft transitional housing by Nickelsville on City of Seattle Property
Penny Lane Village – Muncie, Indiana
Six 96-sq ft houses by Bridges Community Services
Veterans Village – Kansas City, Missouri
Fifty 240 sq ft transitional housing for homeless veterans by Veterans Community Project
14Forward – Marysville, California
Twenty 8'x14' modified Tuff sheds used for emergency (21 days) housing

In the Works

THERE ARE A number of other tiny house villages that are being planned, in progress or recently completed. To the left is a "known" list, meaning there are undoubtedly many more of which we are not aware.

A word of caution: I learned about some of the above projects online just as others discovered the Cass Tiny Homes. Sometimes social media stories are deceptive or even false. For instance, I went to Kansas City to see the four-acre Veterans Community Project. The Facebook video portrayed an occupied and operational village, but the 240 sq. ft. houses weren't even on foundations when I arrived. No one had moved in. Fortunately, the community building was also under construction and the workers graciously showed us the houses. Nonetheless, the video was misleading. They project that the veterans will move in late 2017 and it looks to be a superb program.

Also, the list doesn't include single tiny houses. Habitat for Humanity affiliates have built a few tiny houses across the country. In Michigan, Benjamin Franklin Brown persuaded the Kalamazoo Valley Habitat for Humanity to help him build a 230 sq. ft. house for his retirement. He had served as a volunteer with the Kalamazoo Valley Habitat for several years and the organization turned him down three times before it relented. The build took longer and cost more than the original estimates but Brown's future home is attractive, functional and energy-efficient.

Two other projects deserve special mention as city developments: **A Washington D.C.** community was designed by Boneyard Studios in 2015. The tiny homes in the Stronghold neighborhood are fully off the grid, zero-waste and self-sustaining (photo on page 205). Unfortunately, the project partners have experienced differences and parted ways. Zoning regulations also became an issue.

The other urban project is the result of **cityLAB's 6% experiment**. In 2015, the group started building a 350 sq. ft. house in Garfield, a neighborhood in Pittsburg's east end. The motivation for the project was to attract creative workers to be residents in

Above: The tiny houses in the Washington, D.C. Stronghold neighborhood are all less than 300 sf. Photograph by Tafline Laylin. Used with permission. Below: CityLAB refers to itself as a DO Tank rather than a Think Tank. Their Tiny House on Garfield is evidence of their claim. The 350 sf. house includes a basement with an 8-foot clearance. The architectural plans were done by Wildman Chalmer Design. Photo permission was granted by Electric Lime Studios.

the deteriorating area. Research indicates that if creative workers compose 6% of the population, the neighborhood will experience an economic tipping point. After the construction was complete in 2016, cityLAB sold the property for $109,500 (its asking price).

In contrast, six Amish-built 96-sf. tiny houses in Muncie, Indiana were developed by the Bridges Community Services organization, which is a Community Development Organization commonly referred to as a CHDO. The simple shelters are called Penny Lane (below). There is also a Penny Lane tiny house development underway in North Carolina. It is being built in three phases.

Next Steps at Cass Community

As we continue working to complete the 25 homes of Phase I, some new and exciting partnerships have been established with the **General Motors Foundation**, which has agreed to sponsor three homes for women. We are calling the collaboration Women in Motion, highlighting the Detroit automaker's business and the economic mobility that the tiny homes will create for the low-income residents. GM will send volunteer teams to help with construction in addition to their financial support. **Daniel Libeskind**, who founded an architectural business in New York with his wife, Nina, has offered to design a few tiny homes for Cass. Daniel served as the head of the School of Architecture at Cranbrook Academy in the 1970s and 80s and he went on to do world-renowned buildings such as the Jewish Museum in Berlin, the Royal Ontario Museum in Toronto and the World Trade Center site in Lower Manhattan. Michael Harrison, who interned at the Libeskind Studio and now works at Hamilton Anderson, will assist with the project.

The **Jon Bon Jovi Soul Foundation** contacted us and made a major commitment to the development. **Epitec**, an IT, engineering and staffing organization headed by Jerry and Josie Sheppard, decided to "adopt" six houses as a way to commemorate the company's 40th anniversary. **The Rochester St. Paul's** and the **Midland First United Methodist Churches** have both succeeded in funding tiny homes and we have started discussions with the **Michigan Home Builders** and the **Grosse Pointe Board of Realtors** to see if we can build on the synergy between our organizations.

After the agency completes the first 25 tiny homes for singles and couples, it will move on to a second phase that will pepper the neighborhood with homes for low income families. Data points to a critical shortage of affordable housing options for families in Michigan. The tiny homes will be built slightly larger for these households in order to accommodate bedroom space for the parent(s) and both genders of children. Note: families experiencing homelessness at this time tend to be younger and headed by single-mothers. Children, especially, need housing stability.

The second phase also calls for developing the commercial strip along Woodrow Wilson Street. A mixture of stores and micro enterprise businesses potentially will provide employment for local residents and supply goods and services not yet available within a walking distance. We will simultaneously develop a park to be used for outside social events (concerts, movies, recreational activities including dances, family reunions and staff picnics). Recommendations from the community include drinking fountains and some kind of water feature, a bike rack, a playground, walking/jogging path, benches and picnic tables. There won't be a high ropes course, but you get the idea. We are exploring the possibility of including a memorial garden similar to the one at Community First! Village, as well.

Shrirley ▓▓▓ How good is that
Like · Reply · January 1, 2017 at 6:49am

Kay ▓▓▓ Remember this is a project for a mere 25 units. There are thousands of thousands of homeless, low-income, needy.
Like · Reply · February 12, 2017 at 10:09pm

Karen ▓▓▓ We need this in Australia. Owning ur own home (which is classed as the Aussie dream, only one generation ago) is now mission impossible. Oldies need them too! Cos units are too noisey. Also alot of them have pets as companions n retirement villages don't allow pets.
👍👍👍👍👍
Like · Reply · September 17, 2016 at 10:16pm

Corinne ▓▓▓ This is a beautiful idea oh my God I pray it really happens for the homeless in Detroit and everywhere else I don't believe anyone should have to live on the streets
Like · Reply · January 17, 2017 at 9:32am

Epilogue

MY FATHER TAUGHT economics and history in Detroit Public Schools for thirty years. Among other things, this meant that we talked about the economy and investments at the dinner table most nights and we visited Civil War battlefields while on vacation. After a few semesters of teaching, my dad devised a system to discourage cheating on tests, which proved rather effective. He would give everyone identical questions, but he scrambled them into four different versions. Thus, the same question could appear as #1, 5, 8 and 12 depending on which test a student received. The other questions were likewise arranged in four distinct sequences. That way, if one student copied from another person's paper, it was all but guaranteed that the cheater's answer would be wrong.

After the graded quizzes were returned one afternoon, a boy stayed after the bell rang to complain about his score. Evidently his wandering eyes had earned him a solid "D". The teen protested vehemently for about ten minutes and, then, sensing that he wasn't winning his objection, he blurted out, "I had the right answers. You just asked the wrong questions."

There were days in developing the Tiny Homes at Cass that we could resonate with his statement and frustration. We felt as if the questions and answers were mismatched.

- Why didn't we renovate abandoned buildings?
- Why didn't we require residents to build their own homes?

- Why didn't we just repeat three or four models to keep the costs down?
- Why didn't we squeeze three or four houses onto each lot?
- Why didn't we build "traditional" sized houses, pre-fab houses or shipping container houses?
- Why didn't we make the houses net-zero or completely off the grid?
- Why didn't we stick with seniors or veterans or some other "deserving" population?
- Why didn't we make the houses available for middle-class people who are working hard but unable to afford a mortgage?
- Why didn't we concentrate on raising the minimum wage and/or income inequality?
- Why didn't we design a village or a pocket community with common facilities and/or spaces?

I hope that the chapters of this book answered these questions and others. At the same time, I need to point out that these were not our primary concern. We were pre-occupied with "how" questions, rather than "why" ones.

How could we help poor people obtain an emotional address, a place of relative permanence which would allow them to prosper?

Most of us take this for granted—having a home, that is. In fact, it wasn't until we began working on tiny homes that I really wrestled with what it meant to own a home. As mentioned in the various chapter introductions, I have had the luxury of living in numerous homes.

I was raised on Jane Street on the city's east side with my three brothers. As children, we knew to be home when the streetlights came on. It was where we loved a dog named Sparky, a cat named Rasputin, countless hamsters, two aquariums full of fish as well as our parents and our neighbors.

In Royal Oak, during my teenage years, ours was an accommodating home. My first year of high school, the (pathetic) freshman float for homecoming was assembled in our backyard. Foreign exchange students occupied bedrooms as my older siblings moved out. My eldest brother and his two children came back home before, during and after his divorce. My grandmother Reeves stayed there, too, at the end of her life when she needed around the clock care.

During my years living in dorms at Albion College and apartments around Boston University, when someone asked if I was going home for the holidays or the summer, what they really meant was—are you going to your parent's house in Royal Oak? Home for me then meant a place of retreat, renewal and no-coin laundry appliances. I always drove home for Christmas.

When I was appointed to pastor a church on the west side of Detroit, it came with a house, a parsonage. As much as I loved the property and the autonomy it offered, I was reminded that I was a mere tenant when the trustees opened my drawers and closets each year while conducting their inspections.

Finally, at Cass at forty, I was able to buy a house and, immediately, the old Victorian became my home. The floors weren't level and there wasn't any insulation, but the residence grounded me. Even tackling painting projects and refinishing the hardwood floors made me happy. Then, about a year after I moved into the house in Corktown, my mother called late one night to tell me that my father had died. "Come home," she said. Therein lies the paradox. I was home but I went home.

Through my work at Cass, I have come to know hundreds of people who lack a house but, more importantly, a home. Hence, society refers to them as homeless rather than houseless. Some construct simple structures out of cardboard to avoid the elements and to protect their few possessions. Others sleep under bridges, on park benches, in abandoned buildings or in cars. One of the men I met early on used a discarded tarp to create a tent type of enclosure. He was a veteran who had finished his deployment but never came home. He wasn't at home in his own skin.

Conversely, I have met plenty of seniors and students who have housing but don't have a home. One of our first tiny homes tenants used to stay in a house with her husband. He died prematurely. She was wracked with arthritis and unable to handle the maintenance and repairs of the house. The woman could barely climb the stairs up to the front porch. Beyond that, her neighborhood was overrun with illegal drugs and the gangs that sold them so she became a virtual prisoner.

A second tiny home resident was raised in foster care and at age 18, he was on his own. He "couch surfed" between his sister and several friends for four years. He had a roof, but he was homeless.

Another one of the first tiny homes resident had been incarcerated. By the time he finished his prison sentence, most of his biological family—mother, father, sister and brother—was deceased. He had no one to take him in until he could find employment. What's more, a prison record and the sluggish economy made securing a job problematic.

Dorothy probably summed it up best when she repeated Glinda's words, "There's no place like home." Home is a place where you are surrounded by people, pets, plants and pictures that are important to you. It is where you return to when you have been away at school, are getting a divorce, have been released from the hospital or a prison cell or war. It is where when you pull into the driveway, no matter where you have been—to work or school, a social function or a vacation—you say to yourself, "It's good to be home." I like to say home is where you can get undressed emotionally (even if it means sleeping in the fruit cellar for a while.)

"How could we not only help end homelessness, but how could we assist people to exit poverty?" Put another way, "How could we help people get ahead instead of just getting by?"

I blame Jeffery Sachs. I remember reading his book, "The End of Poverty: Economic Possibilities for Our Time" and realizing that poverty is both stubborn and solvable.[46] His descriptions of extreme poverty (absolute poverty) and moderate poverty provided me an intellectual handle with which to hold the systemic economic, political and social issues pertinent to reducing poverty. The text introduced me to the U.N. Millennial Goals and challenged me to formulate strategies to decrease "relative poverty" domestically.

Of course, the most obvious way to eradicate poverty is to increase the income people receive. It was interesting to us that so many Facebook comments assumed that Cass wasn't addressing income inequality. The

This exterior shot picks up the reflection of the American flag at the Antisdel apartment building, which is close by. Photo by Crystal Fox (theweatheredfox.com).

truth is that our agency has always promoted employment and decent wages with robust benefits. As an agency, we have tried to model this over the years by increasing starting wages, giving annual increases and offering life and health insurance coverage, an incentivized 403 (b) program and tuition re-imbursement for college and graduate courses. There is room for improvement to be sure. Cass pays a living wage for entry level workers who are single but we drop below that standard with the employees who support families. We have intentionally maintained a 3:1 ratio between the the highest paid staff members and those receiving the lowest compensation. We believe in narrowing the income gap and we advocate for the economic security of workers.

The other method of poverty reduction involves asset-creation or the accumulation of wealth. This seemed more impactful for us because it could simultaneously provide financial stability and economic mobility for low income people. Too many adults are trapped financially. According to 2011-2015 census data, one third of the households in the City of Detroit make less than $15,000 a year and 37% of them spend more than 50% of their income on housing.[47]

We decided on tiny home ownership thinking that it would provide a significant asset that would likely appreciate in value over time, in contrast to other items which depreciate, like a car. It was also part and parcel of the American Dream. I have to confess, however, that my thoughts about this have been revised over the last year and a half. People from more than a dozen foreign countries have expressed an interest in replicating the program. Their correspondence strongly suggests that owning a home is a human aspiration rather than one limited to the United States.

"How small is too small?" or "How much space does someone need?"

Years ago Leo Tolstoy wrote a short story, "How Much Land Does a Man Need?"[48] It revolved around a village peasant named Pahom. Pahom believed that if he just had some land, even the devil couldn't stop him. In fact, Tolstoy used the devil to tempt Pahom in the tale, much like Satan conspired against Job. The long and the short of it is that Pahom acquired more and more property, but he wasn't satisfied.

So he traveled to the land of Bashkirs. There, he learned that for 1,000 rubles he could have all of the property that he could walk around in one day, as long as he returned to his starting spot before sunset. Pahom lay awake the night before, calculating how much land he could amass. In the morning, he met up with the chief and the village men before heading out to stake off his land.

It was incredible flat, virgin soil. As the hours passed, the heat affected him. He began to sweat profusely until his clothing was thoroughly soaked. Still, he didn't stop. His mouth was parched and panic set in that he wouldn't make it back in time. Pahom started running. His heart was "beating like a hammer." The sun was about to set. The Bashkirs were yelling at him. With every ounce of his remaining strength, he charged up the hill. His legs buckled under him so that he fell to the ground. His servant rushed to him, tried to raise him, but it was too late. Pahom was dead. Tolstoy ended his classic story by stating that the servant dug a hole and buried Pahom in a six-foot grave and that was all the land that he really needed.

Tolstoy reminds us that we're only on this planet temporarily. Ultimately, we don't require much space. We can extrapolate that we should probably move in the direction of a more minimalistic life. There is wisdom in struggling occasionally with what we need rather than what we want or what we can afford. As you read early on in the book, tiny houses come in a range of sizes, some so small that they should be called tiny bedrooms or a tiny SROs. Cass' development team was conscious of the fact that our residents would be living in the homes for years, compared to months, weeks or days. We didn't want people to feel caged in, as if they'd have to go outside to change their mind. Still, we wanted them small.

One of the highest ranked candidates, a veteran, was shown a few of the first tiny homes at Cass and he decided to decline the program. He said the 325 sf. houses were just too tiny. We moved on to the next person. Living micro is a choice. It is not for everyone. It should probably be avoided if a person's only reason for doing so is financial.

Left to right: The 224 sf. Starlet studio, the 310 sf. Victorian with a loft and the 262 sf. Lighthouse with a garage on the first floor represent some of the size choices. The Chicago house (not pictured) is one of the largest Cass tiny homes at 427 sf. and our only brick exterior.

These California tiny houses are made from recycled materials for people living on the street by Oakland artist Gregory Kloehn. Copyright photo by Brian Reynolds. Used with permission.

"How could we begin re-populating a neighborhood that had lost its gravity?" and "How could people be integrated into the existing community rather than segregating folks out?"

The City of Detroit has 24 square miles of vacant land, over 40,000 blighted structures and another 38,000 which are vacant and soon will join the ranks of ruined buildings. (Note that the nearly 12,000 properties which were demolished between 2014 and 2017 are not included in these figures.)[49] Cass staff members counted over 800 bare lots and abandoned buildings in a mile radius of our headquarters four years ago when we conducted a windshield survey. The physical decay and desertion tends to discourage the residents who have remained in the area. They try to keep up with the yard work on empty adjacent lots but illegal dumping of tires and construction materials is ongoing, making their volunteer landscaping activities demanding. The neighbors

also help board up dangerous buildings. Nevertheless, the blight erodes everyone's property value and invites criminal activity. Thus it was essential to understand that our newest residential program needed to help stabilize the neighborhood. As with everything else related to the Tiny Homes, time and evidence is needed to evaluate the outcome.

How to make the Cass Tiny Homes model sustainable and scalable?

Let me begin by asserting that the use of tiny houses as a (one) solution for people experiencing homelessness has already proven to be inexpensive and practical. The longevity of Dignity Village establishes that it can be sustainable. Even though residential programs always have room for improvement, I would venture to say that each of the village models has components worthy of duplication. For instance, I admired:

- The pioneer role Dignity Village played in establishing stand-alone tiny houses. The individual quarters married dignity and privacy, answering so many of the concerns of LGBTQ people and others who have issues related to living in congregate and often crowded situations.

- The location of Occupy Madison in a city where transportation is readily available and walking is even an option. The proximity to jobs, social services, access to health and mental health care is vital. What's more, the financial commitment of OM's board members is commendable.
- The quality of construction of the tiny houses and community building at Quixote was superior. Their professional staff is also key for chronically homeless men and women.
- In Eugene, I was impressed with the role of self-governance and the way in which Opportunity Eugene was able to convert community opponents to the village into allies in a relatively short period of time. The nationwide set of contacts that Andrew Heben has created in conjunction with SquareOne, the Village Collaborative Network, is impressive.
- I went with some ambivalence thinking that I wouldn't appreciate Community First! given its distance from Austin, but was overwhelmed by the integration of volunteers ("missionaries"), the multiple employment opportunities, street retreats, the memorial garden and Alan's ability to raise millions of dollars to support both phases one and two.
- I haven't yet visited Second Winds but Carmen's recognition that there has to be a place for sexual offenders and his tenacity in terms of emptying the Jungle is exceptional.
- The multi-site arrangement of Nickelsville is noteworthy, as is their collaborative efforts with other capable organizations (including the Low Income Housing Institute and the City of Seattle) which facilitated the transition from unsanctioned camps to city approved programs.
- Hickory Crossing likewise engaged nonprofits, foundations and government offices to create a

residential program that caters to the hardest to reach homeless men and women. They weren't disheartened by a six-year planning period or a $6.8 million dollar price tag.

The Cass Tiny Homes project is a pilot program, an experiment if you will. It may not work or it may need to be modified over time. For instance, some staff members continue to advocate for using a Community Land Trust instead of a Homeowners Association (HOA). Or the tiny homes may surprise all those Facebook comment posters by being wildly successful. It was a risk and I believe in taking risks, especially when the situation is dire. (Again, census data confirms that one third of the households in Detroit have an annual income of $15,000 or less and that they spend an obscene proportion of their monthly money on rent.) My great grandmother doctor took risks too. It was for that reason that my grandfather survived polio and why I am alive today.

Ours was a calculated risk. Our Board of Directors demanded a comprehensive business plan prior to the construction phase and, so, we are reasonably confident that the Cass Tiny Homes will be sustainable. There is a steep learning curve anytime an organization ventures out into new territory, but we developed contingency plans as a part of our model in an effort to stave off unexpected problems. The Cass board also required that the funding needed to be "in the bank" before it could be counted toward the project. Thus, the agency didn't spend money that it didn't have. Just as we avoided government grants, we didn't use loans or lines of credit to build or operate the Tiny Homes.

Scalability is desirable. Twenty-five homes mean nothing when you consider the unmet need for affordable housing and asset creation at the macro level. Tiny homes could provide a viable solution in other major cities. They could also work well in some suburban areas and rural places. Extremely low income people are found everywhere. There are two ways of making this happen. The first requires strategic private fundraising from foundations, corporations, religious communities, schools, individuals, etc. Alan Graham has demonstrated that this approach can support large developments for poor people.

An alternative way to bring about scalability would be to introduce public policy that has the goal of reducing poverty. We, as a nation, have a history of hoisting whole groups of people up into the middle class. When President Roosevelt signed the Social Security Act, 13 million seniors were elevated out of poverty. When President Johnson created Medicare, poverty among the elderly was cut by 2/3rds. When President Clinton expanded the Earned Income Tax, created by Ford and endorsed by Regan, 22 million families escaped poverty.

We likewise have a history of government involvement in home ownership. The G.I. Bill helped veterans secure low- and no-down payment loans and offered longer repayment terms, so that thousands of servicemen and women were able to purchase homes. (The location of the houses and the fact that the program didn't always benefit family farmers or people of color is not lost on the author.) Moreover, year after year, middle-class and upper-class households benefit from mortgage interest deductions. Surely there are policy amendments that would assist extremely poor people. Shortening the time periods for low income housing tax credits (LIHTC) related to tiny home ownership projects would be one such change.

How can tiny homes help with climate change?

Countless people have asked me why we decided on a seven-year rental period. We wanted it to be long enough to insure that the residents were ready to be home owners and not so long as to discourage them in the process. Yet, there is also a spiritual basis for the choice. Seven is symbolic in Scripture. It denotes completeness, wholeness. It is the number of days Genesis identified that God used to finish creation and rest (the model for our week).

I saw a seven-year time frame as a way to link the homes to our concern for the environment, our commitment to take action in response to climate change. Coincidently, the tiny homes, too, remind us that we all live on earth—a tiny home to be sure. Earth is a small planet in the solar system. It is smaller still when looked at as part of the galaxy. It is tiny, lost really, when considering the universe. Yet, it is all we have. At present, anyway, there is no other world for us occupy. We are hopeful, prayerful, that the compact houses will inspire others to deliberately downsize so that our children, grandchildren and great-grandchildren will have a chance to inherit a home that can be inhabited.

Moreover, the number seven is also tied to the concept of sabbatical found in Hebrew Scripture. Every seven years farm land was allowed to rest. It wasn't tilled or planted. After seven sabbatical cycles, according to Leviticus 25, Israel was instructed to observe a time of Jubilee. In fact, the law prescribed that families which had lost their land should receive the original property back after 49 years. (Slaves, too, should be set free according to the same chapter.) This was to prevent a permanent class of poor people. So I chose the number seven.

One final note: Just before my mother moved out of the house in Royal Oak, she called the family home to help her purge. Some things were boxed up for her new apartment. Other items were slated for charity. We were instructed to take anything that belonged to us (like my 25 year-old time capsule high school band sweater) and to pile all of the remaining possessions in at 40-yard commercial dumpster that occupied the driveway. The metal container quickly became an outside junk drawer—spilling over with items my mother knew she would need someday.

When my mother died in 2013, she left my nephew, Jesse, the house on Eleven Mile in Royal Oak. He didn't help build it. He didn't somehow deserve it. She just loved him and wanted to leave him something that could help him and his family have a good life.

Endnotes

1. Holly V. Izard, "Small but Not Forgotten," *Early American Life* (February 2009), 31.

2. Ibid., 33.

3. Henry David Thoreau, *Walden; or, Life in the Woods* (Ticknor and Fields, Boston, Massachusetts, 1854).

4. Donald MacDonald, FAIA, *Democratic Architecture: Practical Solutions to the Housing Crisis* (ORO editions, Gordon Goff, publisher, 2015), 126. Cass Tiny Homes includes a studio cottage by Donald MacDonald.

5. John Steinbeck, *The Grapes of Wrath* (Viking Press, John Lloyd, New York, New York, 1939). The movie based on the book by John Ford starring Henry Fonda was released in 1940.

6. Chris Harring, "Tent City, America," www.placesjournal.org (December 2015).

7. Kathy Weiser, "Hoovervilles of the Great Depression," *Legends of America*, www.legends of America.com/20th-hoovervilles.htlm.

8. Christopher Gray, "Streetscapes: Central Park's 'Hooverville'; Life Along 'Depression Street,'" *The New York Times*, August 29, 1993.

9. "The Great Depression in Washington State: Pacific Northwest Labor & Civil Rights Projects," University of Washington, http://depts.washington.edu/depress/hooverville. shtml.

10. Donald Roy, a sociology student wrote, "Hooverville, a Study of a Community of Homeless Men in Seattle," for his master's thesis in 1935 - http://www.historylink.org/File/2581

11. Jesse Jackson, *The Story of Hooverville, In Seattle*, 1935, https://seattle.gov./cityarchives/exhibits-and-education/ digital-document-libraries/hoovervilles-in-seattle/ excerpt-from-the-story-of-hooverville-in-seattle.

12. Tim O'Neil, "A look back—5,000 settle in shacks along the Mississippi during the Great Depression," toneil@post-dispatch.com, January 3, 2010.

13. "Tent City U.S.A.," Oprah Winfrey Network (OWN) documentary video, 2012. It explores a tent city in Nashville, Tennessee. The DVD is available through Amazon.

14. "No Safe Place: The Criminalization of Homelessness in U.S. Cities," A Report by the National Law Center on Homelessness and Poverty,www.nlchp.org, 2014.

15. Andrew Heben, *Tent City Urbanism: From Self-Organized Camps to Tiny House Villages, the Village Collaborative*, (2014), 27. While focusing on Eugene, Oregon, Heben's book does a superb job in providing details about the existing communities and their histories, as well as offering expert advice about creating new villages. It is available at https://www.squareonevillages.org/.

16. Catherine Mingoya, "Building Together: Tiny House Villages for the Homeless: A Comparative Case Study," 2015, 53. Department of Urban Studies and Planning paper for MIT Master of City Planning degree. Mingoya examined Dignity Village and Occupy Madison. Her work is steeped in research and analysis.

17. The Rev. Dan Bryant, executive director of SquareOne Villages, interview by Faith Fowler. The SquareOne website provided much of the history of Opportunity Village.

18. "Providing for the Unhoused: A Review of Transitional Housing Strategies in Eugene," Final Report, October 2015, was prepared by the Community Planning Workshop (with the University of Oregon). The document demonstrates widespread acceptance from the community and general satisfaction from the people living at Opportunity Village.

19. Heben, *Tent City Urbanism*, 144-155. Outlines the history of and explores questions concerning the use of government funding for Quixote Village.

20. Ginger Segel, "Tiny Houses: A Permanent Supportive Housing Model." White paper released by Community

Frameworks, 2015. It is an excellent resource, describing each phase of Quixote's development.

21. Mingoya, "Building Together," 27.

22. Ibid., 28.

23. Bruce Wellbaum, treasurer of Occupy Madison, interview by Faith Fowler, 2017.

24. Mingoya, "Building Together," 29.

25. Ibid., 36.

26. Stacy Conwell-Leigh, Cass Tiny Homes owner's representative, interview by Carmen Guidi.

27. Sydney O'Shaughnessy, Christie Citranglo, Sarah Chaneles, "Homelessness in Ithaca: A Policy Problem?" *Ithaca Week*, November 14, 2016.

28. Alan Graham with Lauren Hall, *Welcome Homeless: One Man's Journey of Discovering the Meaning of Home* (W. Publishing Group, an imprint of Thomas Nelson, Nashville, Tennessee, 2017).

29. See resident qualifications posted online at http://mlf. org/wp-content/uploads/2015/11/Mobile-Loaves-Resident-Selection-Criteria-11132015.pdf.

30. Hickory Crossing was just fully occupied in March 2017. Thus, most of the information in their section has been gleaned from the website, newspaper articles announcing the groundbreaking and grand opening, and an author interview with a volunteer receptionist.

31. Annie Wiles, "Cottages at Hickory Crossing to House 50 of Dallas' Most Chronically Homeless," *Park Cities People*, September 22, 2016.

32. Greater Seattle Cares provides a layperson's overview of the 11 local encampments in the Puget Sound area. Nickelsville operates four locations: Union, Ballard, Georgetown Tiny House Village and Othello. The city evicted Nickelsville's Dearborn Street encampment while I was visiting in March 2017. SHARE/WHEEL runs four more: Tent City 3, Tent City 4, Tent City 5 and Licton Springs Tiny House Village

(April 2017). Camp Unity Eastside, Camp United We Stand and Camp Second Chance are all independent. http://greaterseattlecares.org/encampments/.

33. Chris Gardner with Quincy Troupe, *The Pursuit of Happyness* (Amistad, an imprint of Harper-Collins Publishers, New York, New York, 2006). The movie co-starring Will Smith as Gardner and Jaden Smith, his biological son, was also released in 2006.

34. Edited by Peter Gavrilovich and Bill McGraw, *The Detroit Almanac* (Detroit Free Press, Inc. Detroit, MI) 477-478. This book manages to sum up the history of Detroit in succinct narrative and bulleted boxes. The chapter that explored the development of the area housing stock was extremely helpful.

35. "Habitat for Humanity Detroit reports layoffs, closures," *The Detroit News* (online), January 17, 2017, updated January 18, 2017.

36. Melvin L. Oliver and Thomas M. Shapiro, "Reducing Wealth Disparities Through Asset Ownership" 142. The essay appears in Ending Poverty in America: How to Restore the American Dream by John Edwards, Marion Crain & Arne L. Kalleberg. The University of North Carolina at Chapel Hill on behalf of the Center for Poverty, Work and Opportunity. Individual essays copyrighted by each author. The New York Press, 2007.

37. Detroit Future City, "139 Square Miles" report (2017) uses housing statistics from the American Community Survey, 2011-2015, which conclude that "58 percent of Detroit renters are cost-burdened, spending more than 30 percent of their income on housing. Thirty-seven percent of Detroit renters spend more than 50 percent of their income on housing."

38. "Fewer homeless veterans. More homeless children in state," www.bridgemi.com(News and analysis from The Center for Michigan), January 12, 2017.

39. The Annie E. Casey Foundation, statistics on aging out at ncsl.org/research/human-services/extending-foster-care-to-18.aspx www.agingoutinstitute.org/what-is-aging-out/.

40. Henri Nouwen and Walter J. Gaffney, *Aging: The Fulfillment of Life* (Image Books, Doubleday imprint, New York, New York, 1976) 23.

41. Armando Delicato and Julie Demery, *Images of America* (Arcadia Publishing, Charleston, South Carolina, 2007) 9.

42. Dan Austin, "Step inside one of Detroit's oldest buildings," *Detroit Free Press*, June 5, 2015.

43. Delicato and Demery, *Images of America*, 126-127.

44. FY 2016 FMR and IL summary system. Geography summary for Detroit-Warren-Michigan. HUD Metro FMR Area.

45. The National Low Income Housing Coalition, *The Gap: A Shortage of Affordable Homes*, Washington, D.C., March 2017.

46 Jeffery Sachs, *The End of Poverty: Economic Possibilities for Our Time,* Penguin Books; Reprint edition (February 28, 2006)

47 Detroit Future City: 139 Square Miles, www.detroitfuturecity.com. August 2017

48 Leo Tolstoy, *How Much Land Does a Man Need?*

49 Detroit Future City, 139 Square Miles, www.detroitfuturecity.com. August 2017

Glossary of Terms/ Acronyms with Web Reference Links

Acquisition

Purchasing a physical site (land and/or buildings) for a housing project.

AMI

The AMI or Area Medium Income is the total household income for the medium housing unit in a region. Each year, Housing and Urban Development (HUD) calculates the AMI for every metropolitan area in the United States. ggwash.org/view/42671/the-area-median-income-ami-explained

CAM

CAM stands for Coordinated Assessment Model. It is a systemic approach to programming for homeless people which aligns their needs with the best program to address those needs. People experiencing homelessness in Detroit initially contact CAM through a call center. camdetroit.weebly.com

Case Management

Case management provides a coordination of services using a single point person/agency. In supportive housing, case management services are designed to offer the tenant support to live independently while establishing or maintaining residential stability. Case management services can include medical and mental health services, substance-abuse services, as well as vocational training or employment services. https://www.hudexchange.info/resources/documents/SHPCaseManagement.pdf

Chronically Homeless

HUD deems a person chronically homeless if she or he has a disability and has been living in a place not meant for human habitation, in an emergency shelter, or a safe haven continuously for the last 12 months OR if she or he has had at least four periods of homelessness in the last three years which cumulatively add up to at least 12 months. csh.org/2015/12/hud-defines-chronically-homeless/

Community Housing Development Organization

A Community Housing Development Organization (CHDO) is a nonprofit, community-based, service organization that has, or intends to obtain, staff with the capacity to develop affordable housing for the community it serves. portal.hud.gov/hudportal/documents/huddoc?id=19790_CHDO.pdf

Community Land Trust

A community land trust is a nonprofit corporation that develops and maintains affordable housing. "CLTs" balance the needs of individuals. https://en.wikipedia.org/wiki/Community_land_trust

Continuum of Care

The Continuum of Care (CoC) was established by HUD (the U.S. Department of Housing and Urban Development) in 1994. It is a process which begins with communities identifying local needs. They then develop strategies to address those needs and submit a single application for the area to HUD in the hopes of funding programs tailored to meet the needs of the community. handetroit.org/continuum-of-care-2/

Diversion Programs

Diversion programs have the goal of assisting people experiencing homelessness before they access shelter services. This includes helping them identify immediate alternative housing arrangements and, if necessary, connecting them with services including monetary assistance, so that they can be quickly returned to permanent housing. http://endhomelessness. org/wp-content/uploads/2011/08/creating-a-successul-diversion-program.pdf

GED

The General Equivalency Diploma (GED) is considered the equivalent of a high school diploma. Prior to taking and passing the battery of tests, people prepare and study usually with an instructor and often for several months. A GED tends to be helpful for those seeking employment/higher education without a traditional high school diploma in that it demonstrates aptitude, knowledge and skills. https://www.gedtestingservice. com/testers/about-ged-test

Gantt Chart

Developed by and named after Henry Gantt, a mechanical engineer, this bar chart shows visually the duration and sequence of the activities which are the essential elements of a project. https://en.wikipedia.org/wiki/Gantt_chart

Homeless

As defined by the U.S. Department of Housing and Urban Development (HUD), persons or families without a fixed, regular, and adequate nighttime residence; or individuals or families that have a primary nighttime residency that is:

- A public or private place not appropriate for human habitation

- A public or privately operated temporary shelter including congregate shelters, transitional housing, hotels/motels paid for by nonprofit organizations or by government agencies.
- This term does not include any individual imprisoned or otherwise detained under an Act of Congress or a State law. https://www.hudexchange.info/resources/documents/HomelessDefinition_RecordkeepingRequirementsandCriteria.pdf

Housing First

A Housing First approach seeks to quickly obtain housing for people experiencing homelessness minus preconditions to services such as sobriety or program participation. Supportive services are made available (but are not mandatory) to help residents maximize housing stability and prevent future episodes of homelessness. This is in contrast to satisfying treatment goals prior to moving into permanent housing. hudexchange.info/resources/documents/Housing-First-Permanent-Supportive-Housing-Brief.pdf

International Building Code

The International Building Code (IBC) was developed by the International Code Council and published in 1997. It is updated every three years. Most states rely on the IBC. It determines standards for fire prevention, finishes, foundations, etc. https://www.iccsafe.org/codes-tech-support/codes/the-i-codes/

Low-Income Housing Tax Credit

The Low-Income Tax Credit (LIHTC) program is currently the country's most extensive affordable housing program. It was added to Section 42 of the Internal Revenue Code in 1986 to encourage property owners to develop and maintain affordable housing units. nhlp.org/lihtcoverview

Permanent Supportive Housing

Permanent Supportive Housing (PSH) is sometimes referred to as just Supportive Housing. It combines non-time-limited affordable housing with voluntary, wrap-around support services.

Project Based Vouchers

A Public Housing Agency (PHA) can enter into a contract with the owner of a building to provide a specified number of units for a specified period of time using Project Based Vouchers. This means that the PHA refers low-income individuals/families to the owner and the owner will be paid the fair market rent for the specified units by combining the renters contribution with the money from the voucher. The voucher stays with the units rather than the renters. portal.hud.gov/hudportal/documents/huddoc?id=DOC_9157.pdf

Rapid Rehousing

Rapid Rehousing connects unhoused people to permanent housing using a tailored package of assistance which may include time-limited financial support and/or targeted services. https://www.hudexchange.info/resources/documents/Rapid-Re-Housing-Brief.pdf

Section Eight Voucher

Section Eight Vouchers are also known as Housing Choice Vouchers. This voucher makes up the difference between what a low-income family pays for rent and the fair market value thus allowing them to rent decent, safe and sanitary housing. The housing must be inspected and pre-approved but families can rent single-family homes, townhouses or apartments using Section Eight. It is not limited to units located in subsidized housing projects. https://affordablehousingonline.com/section-8-housing

Shotgun House

A long narrow house which would allow someone to fire a gun through the front door and have the bullet exit through the back door without ever touching a wall. https://en.wikipedia.org/wiki/Shotgun_house

Single Room Occupancy

Single Room Occupancy (SRO) typically consists of several private living/sleeping rooms and shared kitchen and bathroom facilities. Occasionally an SRO does have a private kitchen and/or bathroom facilities. One or two adults may occupy an SRO unit. https://en.wikipedia.org/wiki/Single_room_occupancy

Stewart McKinney Homeless Act

The Stewart B. McKinney-Vento Homeless Assistance Act is a federal law that was enacted in 1987 and has been reauthorized several times. It provides funding for a spectrum of homeless services. Established by the Interagency Council on the Homeless (now the Interagency Council on Homelessness), it has protections for children experiencing homelessness especially related to education. doi.gov/pam/programs/property_management/McKinney-Vento-HUD-Form

Supplemental Security Income (SSI)

A benefits program enacted as part of the 1972 Social Security Act Amendments and consolidated the Old Age Assistance (OSSA), Aid to the Blind (AB), and Aid to the Permanently and Totally Disabled (APTD) programs. Social Security Income (SSI) is paid monthly to people with low-income, are disabled, or age 65 or older. Children who are visually impaired, disabled or have a deceased parent may also qualify for SSI.

Supportive Services

Supportive services are regularly offered to help residents increase their housing stability. They can include: alcohol/substance abuse services, physical and/or mental health services, independent living skills, vocational services, peer support services and social services.

Ten-Year Plan

In 2000, the National Alliance to End Homelessness published "A Plan, Not a Dream: How to End Homelessness in Ten Years."

The document used the latest research and described some of the most effective programs to outline strategies that could be used locally to address the national issue. http://nlihc.org/sites/default/files/Sec7.08_Ten-Year-Plan_2015.pdf

Transitional Housing

A HUD-funded residential program that has the goal of moving individuals and families into permanent housing within a reasonable amount of time (usually two years). http://peopleof.oureverydaylife.com/definition-hud-transitional-housing-8281.html

VASH

The HUD-Veterans Affairs Supportive Housing (HUD-VASH) program combines Housing Choice Vouchers (aka Section Eight Vouchers) with case management and clinical services for veterans experiencing homelessness through the Department of Veterans Affairs (VA). portal.hud.gov/hudportal/HUD?src=/program_offices/public_indian_housing/programs/hcv/vash

VISPADAT

The Vulnerability Index – Service Prioritization Decision Assistance Prescreen Tool (VI-SPDAT) helps identify who is in the greatest need and who is eligible for housing assistance. orgcode.nationbuilder.com/tools_you_can_use

Yurt

A yurt is a round structure with a self-supporting roof/dome. Traditionally, they were portable and used by nomads. Some modern yurts are permanent buildings on foundations.

Other Resources – Architectural Plans

The blueprints that were done specifically for Cass and gifted to us for sale can be purchased at www.tinyhomesdetroit.org. Funds raised from the sale of these architectural plans are designated for the Tiny Homes development.

The other plans we used were purchased, mostly from Houseplans.com. Houseplans has a wide assortment of tiny houses available to view online and the staff have been very responsive to our questions. Cass bought a couple of the drawings from other outlets like the Perfect Little House Company (perfectlittlehouse.com). In addition to the plans from Perfect Little House, they send a cute ball cap with their logo to thank you for the business.

PHOTOS: (Above) The "Tower Studio" (AKA the Lighthouse) is 262 sf. and has two floors. The ground level is a garage and the upstairs will allow for a 360 degree view of the Cass campus. (Right) The other rendition shows the largest home at Cass. We call it the "Ambassador" and it is 432 sf. There is a loft area for storage but the living space is one level and, as is true for the majority of our homes, there is no garage. Plan images are copyrighted by the original designers, and used with permission from Houseplans.com. The photo of the 300 sf "Tudor" on the cover of this book is also from Houseplans, used with permission.

Additional Print Materials

"Ann Arbor's Kit Homes" by Grace Shackman and Rob Schweitzer, appeared in the Ann Arbor Observer, January 1999 and is at http://aaobserver.aadl.org/aaobserver/36080. This is a wonderful piece that examines the history of kit houses and the people who purchased them/live in them today.

"Tent Cities in America" by the National Coalition for Homeless, March 2010. The publication can be found on the NationalHomeless.org site as can a number of excellent hate crime reports and Discrimination/Criminalization studies.

"The 6% Place" by Eve Picker and cityLAB, was released in November 2011. The document is licensed under a Creative Commons Attribution-NonCommercial-NoDerivs 3.0 Unported License. It offers a condensed version and a longer, comprehensive one both of which tell the story of the tiny house in Pittsburg's Garfield neighborhood.

Tiny House Lodging

Caravan Tiny House Hotel at 5009 NE 11th Street in Portland, Oregon was the first micro lodging in the United States. Today, tiny house accommodations are available across the country - **Austin's Tiny Home Hotel** (Austin, Texas), **Fireside Resort** (Jackson Hole, Wyoming), **Getaway Tiny Homes** (New York and Boston), **Leavenworth Tiny House Village** (Leavenworth, Washington), **Little Chatt** (Chattanooga, Tennessee), **Mt. Hood Tiny House Village** (Mt. Hood, Oregon), **The Village of Wildflowers** (Flat Rock, North Carolina), **Tiny Digs Hotel** (Portland, Oregon), **Yogi Bear's Jellystone Park Tiny Homes** (Virginia, Maryland and Pennsylvania) and **WeeCasa** (Lyons, Colorado). Megan Barber wrote an article in 2016 and revised it July 20, 2017 for Curbed (www.curbed.com/2017/7/20/16003610/tiny-house-hotel-resort) which describes square footage ranges for these hotels, prices, pet policies, builders and contact information.

The Caravan Tiny House Hotel has six different, locally-built homes in Portland Alberta Arts District. The 120-170 sf. houses circle around a common fire pit. The houses have plumbing, electric heat and one is wheelchair accessible.

Sarah M. Murphy rents out her own tiny house as an Airbnb. She is a consultant for tiny house hospitality. Her web site http://www.tinyhousehotelie.com/ offers some free resources/tools about building, branding, pricing, customer service as well as contact information to book a consultation.

Videos

Camp Take Notice, Ann Arbor, MI (2015) – https://www.youtube.com/watch?v=uFRZIS_tXqQ

36 minute documentary by Vivianna Pernot, a University of Michigan Stamps School of Art and Design student.

DOORWAYS TO DIGNITY – http://www.kwamba.com/documentary.doorways.html

Kwamba Productions slideshow photos of Dignity Village. Also provides a link to information about a Kickstarter campaign to raise funds to finish DOORWAYS TO DIGNITY, a feature-length documentary about the history and struggles of the program by filmmakers Kohn and Mosher who collected 600+ hours of footage and photos.

Nickelsville (2016) – https://www.youtube.com/watch?v=oedKozxmg3w&feature=youtu.be

8 minutes, 23 second overview of the Nickelsville Tiny Houses

The Ithaca Jungle (2013) – https://www.youtube.com/watch?v=Oxw94GgVxRI

13 minutes Carmen Guidi gives an informal tour (the sound is poor but the visuals are instructive).

We The Tiny House People (Documentary): Small Homes, Tiny Flats & Wee Shelters (2012) – https://www.youtube.com/watch?v=lDcVrVA4bSQ

1 hour, 21 minutes by Kirsten Dirksen - takes a look at tiny homes internationally

Acknowledgements

AS ALWAYS, I am indebted to countless individuals and organizations for making my work possible. This book wouldn't have been written without the spotlight that social media brought to our tiny homes project and, so, let me begin by thanking Mark Zuckerberg, David Wolfe and the production team from NowThis Future.

It couldn't have been written without a sabbatical leave provided by the McGregor Fund and approved by the Cass Board of Directors.

It never would have been published without the financial backing of the Bath Family Foundation. In addition, I have relied on the wise counsel of Clifford Bath for years. He has the gift of quietly making dreams come true.

I am deeply grateful for all of the philanthropists who have contributed to the construction of the tiny homes, especially those who provided financial support in the early stages of the project—the RNR Foundation and the Ford Fund. It has been a privilege to have partners and friends like Richard Lord, Sue Jeffers and Jim Vella.

Michelle Phellps ably assisted with the research for Tiny Homes In a Big City, thus extending my reach into the stacks at the Main Detroit Public Library and countless pages and posts on the Internet.

Many friends endured this experience and even served as readers of multiple versions of the narrative including Judy Harnish, Gayle McGarvah, Kim Hudolin, Robin Budd, Pat

McCaffrey-Green, Ed Hingelberg, Jeanette Harris, Carol Goll, Charmaine Kunz, Terra Linzner, Louise Travis and Spencer Hayes.

Cass interns Amanda Funk and Ashlee Williams scrolled through thousands of posts in order to ferret out the best samples for inclusion in the book and former intern Tashon McDuffie was the principal photo researcher, obtaining permission to use copyrighted pictures from multiple sources.

Graphic designer Dick DeRonne glimpsed the promise of the book and contributed a brilliant cover and many of the internal charts and artistic layouts.

Marcy Hayes, whose constancy and vivid presence has helped me for over 15 years now, provided sound advice when we were confronted with thousands of requests, media and otherwise.

We appreciate all of the access and information from each of the Tiny House Villages. They have been the pioneers of using micro housing and many of their leaders have fought for the advances we are now beginning to see in terms of zoning and minimum housing requirements.

Dmitri Barvinok and all the other mentors and muses at Front Edge Publishing deserve our thanks.

Finally, I need to apologize for stealing so much of the limelight when at least three people have worked tirelessly behind the scenes to turn a vision into reality—Stacy Conwell-Leigh, who prodded the professionals and took charge of security, Loren Sohn, who stepped in and supervised an army of both skilled and unskilled volunteers and Sue Pethoud, who organized everything and everyone else while gently pushing me to meet the deadlines.

About the Author

Marisa ████ Who is behind this non profit?
Let's find out how legitimate this group is!!!!!
Like · Reply · September 17, 2016 at 12:03pm

Rev. Faith Fowler sold her 1864 Victorian home in Corktown in order to live in the Tiny Home neighborhood as it was being established. In 2016, she sold an investment property and purchased a 1973, 1,400 sq. ft. (including the attached garage) ranch on Lake Huron. She plans to live "happily ever after" in significantly smaller residences. This is her second book.

Rev. Fowler has been the pastor at Cass Community United Methodist Church and the Executive Director of Cass Community Social Services since 1994. The Cass congregation dates back to 1881 and the nonprofit programs were started during the Great Depression.

s took this photo of Rev. Fowler in front of the
on Elmhurst. It is used with permission.

ιomes In a Big City

About Cass Community Social Services

Zakiyyah ▦▦▦ I think that is a beautiful thing that they are doing in Detroit Michigan for the homeless people God bless the people who are involved in this project
Like · Reply · September 16, 2016 at 6:29am

Cass Community Social Services (Cass) provides food, housing, health care/mental health care and jobs for people living in areas of concentrated poverty in Detroit. The 501 (c) (3) nonprofit does this using a pedestrian campus so that residents can easily access a wide variety of services, including educational classes, recreational facilities, community meals, a medical clinic, a library, fellowship (sobriety) groups and jobs. ALL of the services are optional and free.

About the Cass Community Publishing House

Timothy ▦▦▦ If anybody knows the link I can go to the look up this stuff better can and somebody send it to me please that's a really good idea and I really want to look into that more please please please please
Like · Reply · September 14, 2016 at 9:19am

CCPH was established in 2013. It was the first ecumenical publishing house based in Detroit since the Catholic pioneer Father Gabriel Richard hauled the first printing press into the city and began publishing in 1809. The Cass Publishing House has the goals of spotlighting urban issues and/or religious ideas and providing a platform for underrepresented voices.

If you want to request a speaker or to arrange for a consultation, Rev. Fowler can be reached through the web site www.casscommunity.org. If you want to support the Tiny Homes project financially, donations can be made online at www. casscommunity.org or sent to Cass Community Social Services, 11745 Rosa Parks, Detroit, MI 48206. Please indicate that the money is earmarked for Tiny Homes using the memo line. If you would like information about including Cass Community Social Services in estate plans, call (313) 883-2277, ext. 201.

About the Author •